Lecture Notes of the Institute for Computer Sciences, Soc and Telecommunications Er

T0092344

Anastasios Doulamis   Joe Mambretti
Ioannis Tomkos   Theodora Varvarigou (Eds.)

Networks
for Grid Applications

Third International ICST Conference, GridNets 2009
Athens, Greece, September 8-9, 2009
Revised Selected Papers

 Springer

Volume Editors

Anastasios Doulamis
Technical University of Crete
Kounoupidiana, 73132 Chania Crete, Greece
E-mail: adoulam@cs.ntua.gr

Joe Mambretti
Northwestern University
International Center for Advanced Internet Research
750 North Lake Shore Drive,
Chicago, IL 60611, USA
E-mail: j-mambretti@northwestern.edu

Ioannis Tomkos
Athens Information Technology Centre
PO Box 68, Peania 19002 Athens, Greece
E-mail: itom@ait.edu.gr

Theodora Varvarigou
ICCS, National Technical University
Heroon Polytechniou 9 str
157 73 Athens, Greece
E-mail: Dora@telecom.ntua.gr

Library of Congress Control Number: 2009943613

CR Subject Classification (1998): C.2, H.3.4, H.2.4, C.2.4, D.4.3, D.1.3, D.4.7

ISSN   1867-8211
ISBN-10   3-642-11732-5 Springer Berlin Heidelberg New York
ISBN-13   978-3-642-11732-9 Springer Berlin Heidelberg New York

springer.com

© ICST Institute for Computer Sciences, Social-Informatics and Telecommunications Engineering 2010
Printed in Germany

Typesetting: Camera-ready by author, data conversion by Scientific Publishing Services, Chennai, India
Printed on acid-free paper   SPIN: 12987719   06/3180   5 4 3 2 1 0

Preface

The GridNets conference is an annual international meeting that provides a focused and highly interactive forum where researchers and technologists have an opportunity to present and discuss leading research, developments, and future directions in grid networking. The goal of this event is to serve as both the premier conference presenting best grid networking research and a forum where new concepts can be introduced and explored.

After the great success of the Second International Conference on Networks for Grid Applications in Beijing, China, which was held during October 8–9, 2008, the next event was scheduled for Athens in 2009. The 2009 event featured two invited keynote speakers, ten reviewed papers, and three invited papers. The program was supplemented by forums on three key areas—a workshop on Green Grids, a workshop on Wireless Grids, and a workshop on Optical Grids.

Next year's event is currently being planned, and it will incorporate multiple new important emerging topics related to grid networks.

December 2009

Tasos Doulamis
Joe Mambretti
Ioannis Tomkos
Dora Varvarigou

Organization

Steering Committee Chair

Imrich Chlamtac   CREATE-NET, Italy

Conference General Co-chairs

Ioannis Tomkos   Athens Information Technology, Greece
Joe Mambretti   Northwestern University, USA

Conference Organization Chair

Gergely Nagy   ICST

Local Co-chairs

Konstantinos Kanonakis   Athens Information Technology, Greece
Dimitrios Klonidis   Athens Information Technology, Greece
Yvan Pointurier   Athens Information Technology, Greece

Program Committee Co-chairs

Dora Varvarigou   NTUA, Greece
Tasos Doulamis   Technical University of Crete, Greece

Publicity Co-chairs

Sumit Naiksatam   Cisco, USA
Serafim Kotrotsos   EXIS I.T., Greece

Publication Chair

Stelios Sartzetakis   GRNet, Greece

Workshops Chair

Emmanouel Varvarigos   RACTI, Greece

Webmasters

Georgia Pispirigou   Athens Information Technology, Greece
Yvan Pointurier   Athens Information Technology, Greece

Technical Program Committee

Bill Allcock   Argonne National Lab (USA)
Olivier Audouin   Alcatel-Lucent Bell Labs (France)
Siamak Azodolmolky   AIT (Greece)
Micah Beck   University of Tennessee (USA)
Piero Castoldi   CNIT (Italy)
Chris Develder   IBBT (Belgium)
Christopher Edwards   Lancaster University (UK)
Silvia Figueira   Santa Clara University (USA)
Gabriele Garzoglio   Fermi National Accelerator Laboratory (USA)
Paola Grosso   University of Amsterdam (The Netherlands)
Yunhong Gu   University of Illinois at Chicago (USA)
Wei Guo   Shanghai Jiao Tong University (China)
Jun He   Texas State (USA)
Doan Hoang   University of Technology, Sydney (Australia)
David Hutchison   Lancaster University (UK)
Jussi Kangasharju   University of Helsinki (Finland)
Rajkumar Kettimuthu   The University of Chicago/Argonne National La (USA)
Dieter Kranzlmueller   GUP-Linz (Austria)
Laurent Lefevre   INRIA (France)
Tiejun Ma   University of Oxford (UK)
Joe Mambretti   Northwestern University (USA)
Olivier Martin   ICT Consulting (Switzerland)
Andreas Menychtas   NTUA (Greece)
Christine Morin   INRIA (France)
Anand Padmanabhan   University of Iowa (USA)
Marcelo Pasin   ENS-Lyon/INRIA (France)
Nicholas Race   Lancaster University (UK)
Elio Salvadori   Create-NET (Italy)
Nicola Sambo   SSSUP (Italy)
Chava Saradhi   Create-NET (Italy)
Jane Simmons   Monarch Networks (USA)
Zhili Sun   University of Surrey (UK)
Dominique Verchere   Alcatel-Lucent (France)
Michael Welzl   University of Innsbruck (Austria)
Oliver Yu   University of Illinois at Chicago (USA)
Wolfgang Ziegler   Fraunhofer-Gesellschaft (Germany)
Dimitris Zisiadis   University of Thessaly (Greece)

Green Grids Workshop Chair Information

Chris Develder   Ghent University, Belgium
Mario Pickavet   Ghent University, Belgium

Wireless Grids Workshop Organizing Committee / TPC

Hassan Charaf   Budapest University of Technology and Economics,
                                   Hungary
Frank H.P. Fitzek   Aalborg University, Denmark
Marcos D. Katz   VTT, Finland
Lee McKnight   Syracuse University, USA
William Lehr   MIT, USA
Lutz Schubert   University of Stuttgart, German

Optical Grids Workshop Chair Information

Kyriakos Vlachos   University of Patras, Greece
Dominique Verchere   Alcatel-Lucent, France

Table of Contents

Green Grids Workshop

Wireless Grids Workshop

Designing 21st Century Communications: Architecture, Services, Technology, and Facilities

Joe Mambretti

International Center for Advanced Internet Research, Northwestern University (iCAIR.org),
Metropolitan Research and Education Network (www.mren.org)
j-mambretti@northwestern.edu

Abstract. Increasing demand for new applications and services, continuous technology innovation, and rapidly changing economics are motivating the creation of a fundamentally new architecture for 21st century digital communications. Traditional architectural models for communications have been oriented toward meeting exacting requirements of a finite set of well-defined services, essentially, a fixed set of modalities, with well known and well defined parameters. Consequently, this infrastructure has become a restrictive barrier to the deployment of new and enhanced services and capabilities. Meeting the many requirement challenges of continual change requires replacing traditional rigid designs with those that are significantly more flexible and customizable. Often, advances in networking are measured only by increased capacity, and certainly substantially more capacity is required. Fortunately, advanced optical technologies have been created to support 100 Gbps and higher capabilities. However, high capacity alone does not guarantee high performance, and high performance capability does not guarantee required flexibility and determinism. Today, new types of digital communications infrastructure are being designed, prototyped, and provisioned in early implementations. These new design provide for a foundation infrastructure consisting of discoverable, reconfigurable resources that can be dynamically integrated and used. This infrastructure can be considered a programmable platform that can support many more services than traditional deployments, including highly differentiated and deterministic services.

Introduction

Today, there is an unprecedented increase in demand for many types of new applications and services along with accelerating increases in requests for enhancements and extensions of existing applications and services. At the same time, continuous technology innovation is providing many new capabilities, functions, tools and methods, which provide exciting new opportunities to create powerful advanced applications and services. Another macro trend is the changing economics of communications, which is substantially lowering costs at all levels, especially component costs. These decreasing costs allow for more capabilities to be implemented among many additional communities and geographic areas. Collectively, these macro trends are motivating a substantially new architecture for 21st century digital communications.

T. Doulamis et al.: (Eds.): GridNets 2009, LNICST 25, pp. 1–6, 2010.

The traditional architectural development model for communications has been motivated toward meeting the exacting requirements of a finite set of one or a few well-defined services, essentially, a fixed set of modalities, with well known and well defined parameters. This approach leads to the creation of infrastructure that is highly restrictive. Basically, such infrastructure is created to support a few functions extremely well rather than a wide range of capabilities. Furthermore, this infrastructure has been designed and implemented for extremely long lifecycles, with an expectation that major changes would not be implemented for many years. Changes would be undertaken as significant, costly upgrades at a fundamental level. This traditional approach constitutes a substantial barrier to deploying of new and enhanced applications and services.

Meeting the many requirement challenges of continual change requires replacing traditional designs with those that are significantly more flexible and innovative. These new designs provide for a foundation infrastructure consisting of discoverable, reconfigurable resources that can be dynamically integrated, used, and then returned to a resource repository.

These designs provide for communications infrastructure that basically constitutes a large scale distributed programmable platform that can be used to design, implement and operate many types of services, far more than the few based on traditional communication infrastructure deployments, including highly customizable, differentiated and deterministic services. These new designs enable the design, provisioning, and customization of an almost unlimited number of services. These designs provide for not a single centrally controlled network but instead a large scale, distributed facility - - a highly decentralized environment, within which it is possible to create many different networks, each with distinctive characteristics, and each capable of numerous individualized services. These concepts are natural extensions of basic Grid models, i.e., distributed programmable computing environments. Today, the majority of Grids use undifferentiated networks. However, Grid networks extend the Grid concept to network services and infrastructure, creating capabilities for directly addressable programmable networks [1].

Requirement Challenges

Clearly, there are many requirement challenges related to next generation network services. For example, even though there has been much progress in convergence, various major communication service modalities such as voice, video, wireless, and data are still deployed on separate infrastructure, supported by different protocols and technologies. The current, Internet primarily provides a single best effort undifferentiated service, which provides only minimal support for digital media. Traditional Internet architecture and protocols will be challenged as it scales from a service for just over one billion individuals to one that can support over three billion individuals. For example,, Internet security problems are well known as are problems with supporting individual large scale data streams. [2]

These are a few requirements for current general data networking. To preview future networking, it is useful to observe the challenges encountered by large scale data intensive and compute intensive science applications. [3] Large scale, data intensive science applications tend to encounter technology barriers years before they are encountered by other communities. Therefore, the issues that they encounter and the responses to them provide a useful looking glass into the future. Today, one major issue for such applications is bandwidth capacity. Many applications require the gathering, analysis and transport of petabytes of data. Another requirement is a need for dynamic provisioning at all network layers. Another cross cutting requirement at all levels is programmability. Capabilities are required for enabling determinism is be controlled by edge devices.

Meeting Bandwidth Capacity Requirements

Providing for capacity requirements is a particularly interesting issue. Today, there are major on-going increases in capacity demands. Often, advances in networking are measured only by increased capacity. Fortunately, advanced optical technologies have been created to support extremely high volume capacities, including 100 Gbps and higher. [4, 5] These capabilities are beginning to be deployed today. However, high capacity alone does not guarantee high performance, and high performance capability does not guarantee required flexibility and determinism. To fully optimally utilize such capacity, it will be necessary to address a range of issues related to architectural designs, provisioning methods, signally, core components, and others.

New Architectural Designs for Communications

Despite the difficulty and complexity of these challenges, new communications architectural designs methods are being created for meeting them. [1] These designs represent a fundamentally transformation of the traditional models. In the past, many of the most challenging problems in information technology have been addressed by creating architecture and technology that provides for a higher level of abstraction than those used by the current generation. This basic and proven approach is being used to design new architecture for communication services and infrastructure.

Some of these techniques are leveraging developments in other areas of information technology. For example, Services Oriented Architecture (SOA) is being widely used to enhance general services provisioning on distributed and data center infrastructure. SOA enables resources to be highly customized and fine tuned using granulated component identification, selection, integration, and partitioning. Today, a number of networking research organizations are creating customizable SOA based models for communication services, especially to match precisely requirements at different sites with customized services.

Another area of leveraging is the trend toward implementing virtualized services, which mitigate or eliminate restrictions of local implementations and configurations, especially physical hardware. Virtualization transforms infrastructure from rigid physical resources to sets of individual software objects, enabling the creating of distributed programmable platforms. Virtualization can significantly enhance communication services by decoupling services from specific implementations and configurations of underlying hardware and software. Virtualization provides high levels of flexibility in resource discovery, selection, integration, application, reconfiguration, customization, and response to changing conditions.

At the same time that these architectural models are being developed, technology innovations continue to advance at an accelerating rate. New protocols are being created, as are new types of signaling, switching fabrics, routing functions, appliances, optical transport components, and many other innovations. The large range of new innovations gives rise to a reconsideration of the traditional network architectural model.

Deep and Wide 4D Networking

The traditional network architectural model is based on a hierarchical set of defined layers, which for many years has assisted in formulating contextual framework descriptions of the relative placement and relationship of services and functions. Over the last few years, this basic model has been challenged as recent architectural concepts have proposed new types of mid-layer services, processes that enable non-hierarchical transitions among layers, increasingly sophisticated and complex services at each layer, and many more types of services at each layer. If the traditional OSI seven layer model could be considered a horizontal axis, the additional services at each layer could be considered a vertical axis. For example, today many variant transport protocol stacks are being created. It is possible to consider them not as mutually exclusive but as potentially selectable options, resources within a highly distributed programmable communications environment. Individual services could dynamically select specific transport protocols from among multiple available options. Variations among those services could be considered a third (Y) axis, resulting in a 3D model of functionality. The fourth dimension, time, is important to note because of the increasing implementation of dynamic provisioning capabilities at all layers, including dynamic lighpath provisioning. For example, over the last few years, capabilities for dynamic lightpath provisioning have been significantly advanced. [6,7,8] Traditionally, services at different layers and using different protocols have been fairly compartmentalized. However, using new types of abstraction techniques, it is possible to envision high level services being created by combining multiple layers of services and protocols, and even creating those services dynamically and continually adjusting them as requirements and conditions change.

Dynamic Services Provisioning

The benefits of this new model can be demonstrated by noting the advantages of dynamic services provisioning. An especially challenging communication services issue has been providing support for large scale high volume individual data flows while maintaining fairness to other much smaller sized flows. Because traditional data services and infrastructure are designed to support large numbers of individual data flows, managing single high volume flow is problematic. However, using new architectural models that can effectively dynamically reprogram core resources, it is possible to provide services for such data intensive streams, including at the petascale and terascale level.

Edge Signaling

Another implication of this model is that it will enable much more functionality and capabilities at edge sites. This model allows for transition from highly centralized hierarchical management and control systems to highly distributed management and control. Therefore, instead requiring edge sites processes to accept generalized communication services as only designed and delivered, the new approach will provide them with options for customizing those services to meet precise local requirements. In fact, this architecture will allow edge site to create their own customized services using core resources as fundamental building blocks.

Testbeds and Early Prototype Implementations

This new architectural model is being investigated using multiple local, national, international advanced network research testbeds, including by Grid network research communities. However, it is already emerging from research organizations and it is beginning to be implemented within metro, national, and international prototype facilities. These facilities are being used to demonstrate a wide spectrum of innovative, high performance large-scale applications, advanced data services, and specialized networks. Examples of early implementations consist of innovative high performance Grid networks, Cloud networks, such as the Open Cloud Testbed (www.ncdm.uic.edu), science research networks, digital media networks, and extremely large scale high performance computing networks. [9,10,11]

Several national governments world-wide have funded large scale implementations of next generation network testbeds and prototypes. In the US, the National Lambda Rail (NLR) is a national scale distributed facility based on lightpaths supported by an optical network using fiber leased by a university consortium (www.nlr.net). The NLR supports multiple large scale testbeds, including many that are developing new types of high performance services. Internationally, the Global Lambda Integrated Facility (GLIF) is a large scale distributed facility based on lightpaths supported by optical networks provisioned among several continents (www.glif.is). The core nodes of the GLIF consist of multiple international exchange points, facilities that interconnect regional, national, and international research and education networks, and a few corporate research networks. One such facility, the StarLight international communications exchange on the Chicago campus of Northwestern University provides support for over 80 10 Gbps lightpaths interconnecting sites in the metro area, across the state, regionally, nationally and world-wide (www.startap.net/starlight). StarLight is being used to design, implement, and operate multiple innovative advanced communication services for a wide range of advanced applications.

Summary

Emerging 21st communication applications and services have much more aggressive requirements than those that are commonly deployed today. Future applications and services will be much more powerful, flexible, customizable, and reliable. To provide these benefits, fundamentally new communication services and infrastructure architectural models must be created and deployed. Today, in response to these challenges, early architectural concepts are being designed, investigated, and implemented in prototype. The early results demonstrated by these prototypes have indicated that the new architectures models will provide a wide range of new benefits.

References

[1] Travostino, F., Mambretti, J., Karmous-Edwards, G. (eds.): Grid Networks: Enabling Grids with Advanced Communication Technology. Wiley, Chichester (2006)

[2] Gu, Y., Grossman, R.: UDT: UDP-based data transfer for high-speed networks. Computer Networks 51(7) (May 2007)

[3] Special Issue, Journal of Future Generation Computer Systems 22(8) (October 2006)

[4] Mambretti, J., Aoyama, T.: Report of the Interagency Optical Networking Testbed Workshop 3, Networking and Information Technology Research and Development's Large Scale Network Coordinating Group (May 2007)

[5] Petravick, D., Bill Wing, N.G.J.M., Yu, N.R.D.: US Department of Energy Office of Science. In: Workshop Report on Advanced Networking for Distributed Petascale Science: R&D Challenges and Opportunities, April 8-9 (2008)

[6] Mambretti, J., Lillethun, D., Weinberger, J.: Optical Dynamic Intelligent Network Services (ODIN): An Experimental Control Plane Architecture for High Performance Distributed Environments Based on Dynamic Lightpath Provisioning. IEEE Communications 44(3), 92–99 (2006)

[7] Lillethun, D., Lange, J., Weinberger, J.: Simple Path Control Protocol Specification, IETF draft-lillethun-spc-protocol-00.txt

[8] DeFanti, T., Brown, M., Leigh, J., Yu, O., He, E., Mambretti, J., Lillethun, D., Weinberger, J.: Optical Switching Middleware For the OptIPuter, Special Issue on Photonic IP Network Technologies for Next-Generation Broadband Access. IEICE Transactions on Communications E86-B(8), 2263–2272 (2003)

[9] DeFanti, T., De Laat, C., Mambretti, J., St Arnaud, B.: TransLight: A Global Scale Lambda Grid for E-Science. Special Issue on Blueprint for the Future of High Performance Networking, Communications of the ACM 46(11), 34–41 (2003)

[10] Smarr, L., Chien, A., DeFanti, T., Leigh, J., Papadopoulos, P.: The OptIPuter. Special Issue: Blueprint for the Future of High Performance Networking Communications of the ACM 46(11), 58–67 (2003)

[11] Mambretti, J.: Progress on TransLight and OptIPuter and Future Trends Towards Lambda Grids. In: Proceedings, Eighth International Symposium on Contemporary Photonics Technology (CPT 2005), Tokyo, January 12-14 (2005)

Part I

General Session 1

Authorisation Infrastructure for On-Demand Grid and Network Resource Provisioning

Yuri Demchenko[1], Mihai Cristea[1], Cees de Laat[1], and Evangelos Haleplidis[2]

[1] University of Amsterdam, System and Network Engineering Group
{demch,cristea,delaat}@science.uva.nl
[2] University of Patras
ehalep@gmail.com

Abstract. The paper presents the Authorisation (AuthZ) infrastructure for combined multidomain on-demand Grid and network resource provisioning which we refer to as the Complex Resource Provisioning (CRP). The proposed CRP model provides a common abstraction of the resource provisioning process and is used as a basis for defining the major AuthZ mechanisms and components that extend the generic AAA AuthZ framework to support CRP (GAAA-CRP), in particular using XML-based AuthZ tickets and tokens to support access control and signalling during different CRP stages. The proposed GAAA-CRP framework is implemented as the GAAA Toolkit pluggable library and allows integration with the Grid and network service and control plane middleware. The proposed authorisation infrastructure allows using in-band binary tokens to extend network access control granularity to data plane and support binding applications to dataflows. The paper discusses the use of the ForCES network management model to achieve interoperability with the network control plane and define the GAAA-NRP interfaces to network control plane. This research was conducted as a part of the EU Phosphorus project.

Keywords: Complex Resource Provisioning (CRP), Multidomain Network Resource Provisioning, AAA Authorisation Framework, Authorisation session, Token Based Networking (TBN), ForCES.

1 Introduction

High performance distributed Grid applications that deal with high volume of processing and visualisation data require dedicated high-speed network infrastructure provisioned on-demand. Currently large Grid projects and Cloud Computing providers use their own dedicated network infrastructure that can handle the required data throughput but typically are over-provisioned. Any network upgrade or reconfiguration still requires human interaction to change or negotiate a new Service Level Agreement and involve network engineers to configure the network. Need for combined computer-network resources provisioning and optimisation will increase with emerging Cloud Computing that has stronger commercial focus than Grid computing.

Most of Grid usage scenarios can benefit from combined Grid and network resource provisioning that besides improving performance can address such issues as

T. Doulamis et al.: (Eds.): GridNets 2009, LNICST 25, pp. 9–18, 2010.

(application centric) manageability, consistency of the security services and currently becoming important energy efficiency. The combined Grid/computer and network resource provisioning requires that a number of services and network resources controlling systems interoperate at different stages of the whole provisioning process. However in current practice different systems and provisioning stages are not connected in one workflow and can not keep provisioning and security context, what is resulted in a lot of manual work and many decision points that require human involvement.

In this paper we extend the proposed earlier the Network Resource Provisioning (NRP) model [1] to the more general Complex Resource Provisioning (CRP) model that provides a common framework for combined Grid/computer resources and network infrastructure provisioning and allows for integrating existing systems/ services and technologies into common provisioning workflow that include such stages as reservation, deployment, access, and additionally decommissioning, that require different security and access control services and mechanisms.

Security and authorisation services to support CRP should have high granularity, capable of dynamic invocation at different networking layers, and support all stages of the provisioned resources lifecycle. The proposed GAAA-CRP infrastructure and services are designed in such a way that they can be used at all networking layers (dataflow plane, control plane and service plane) and allow easy integration with Grid middleware and application layer security. For this purpose, special mechanisms are proposed to manage inter-layer and inter-domain security context.

The paper is organized as follows. Section 2 describes the proposed general CRP model that separates resource reservation, resource deployment, and resource access stages. This section also summarises common requirements to AuthZ services/ infrastructure to support different provisioning and AuthZ scenarios in distributed dynamic environment. Section 3 discusses the use of the AuthZ tickets and tokens for signalling and access control in multidomain CRP. Section 4 provides suggestions how the ForCES and Token Based Networking (TBN) can be used to achieve higher granularity of the control of the provisioned network paths. Section 5 briefly presents our ongoing implementation, and finally section 6 provides a short summary and suggests future developments.

2   CRP Model and GAAA-CRP Authorisation Infrastructure

The typical on-demand resource provisioning process includes four major stages, as follows: (1) resource reservation; (2) deployment (or activation); (3) resource access/ consumption, and additionally; (4) resource de-commissioning after it was used. In its own turn, the reservation stage (1) typically includes three basic steps: resource lookup; complex resource composition (including alternatives), and reservation of individual resources.

The reservation stage may require the execution of complex procedures that may also request individual resources authorisation. This process can be controlled by an advance reservation system [2] or a meta-scheduling system [3]; it is driven by the provisioning workflow and may also include Service Level Agreement (SLA) negotiation [4]. At the deployment stage, the reserved resources are bound to a reservation ID, which we refer to as the Global Reservation Identifier (GRI). The decommissioning stage is considered as an important stage in the whole resource provisioning workflow from the provider point of view and should include such important actions as global provisioning/access session termination and user/process logout, log information sealing, accounting and billing.

The rationale behind defining different CRP workflow stages is that they may require and can use different security models for policy enforcement, trust and security context management, but may need to use common dynamic security context.

In the discussed CRP model we suggest that the resources are organised in domains that are defined (as associations of entities) by a common policy or a single administration, with common namespaces and semantics, shared trust, etc. In this case, the domain related security context may include:

- static security context such as domain based policy authority reference, trust anchors, all bound by the domain ID and/or domain trust anchor [19];
- dynamic or session related security context bound to the GRI and optionally to a Local Reservation ID (LRI).

In general, domains can be hierarchical, flat or have irregular topology, but all these cases require the same basic functionality from the access control infrastructure to manage domain and session related security context. In the remainder of the paper we will refer to the typical use case of the network domains that are connected as chain (sequentially) providing connectivity between a user and an application.

Figure 1 illustrates major interacting components in the multi-domain CRP using example of provisioning multidomain network connectivity between a User and a Destination resource or application. Each networking domain is presented as

- Network Elements (NE) (related to the network Data plane);
- Network Resource Provisioning Systems (NRPS) acting as a Domain Controller (DC) (typically related to the Control plane);
- Inter-Domain Controller (IDC) managing cross-domain infrastructure operation, often referred to as Network Service Plane (NSP).

Access to the resource or service is controlled by the DC or NRPS and protected by the generic Authentication, Authorisation, Accounting (AAA) service that enforces a resource access control policy. The following functional elements comprise the proposed authorisation infrastructure for CRP which we will refer to as GAAA-CRP:

- Policy Enforcement Point (PEP), Policy Decision Point (PDP), and Policy Authority Point (PAP) as major functional components of the Generic AAA AuthZ infrastructure (GAAA-AuthZ) [5].
- Token Validation Services (TVS) that allow efficient authorisation decision enforcement when accessing reserved resources.

Depending on the basic GAAA-AuthZ sequence (push, pull or agent) [4], the requestor can send a resource access request to the resource (which in our case is represented by NRPS) or an AuthZ decision request to the designated AAA server which in this case will act as a PDP. The PDP identifies the applicable policy or policy set and retrieves them from the PAP, collects the required context information,

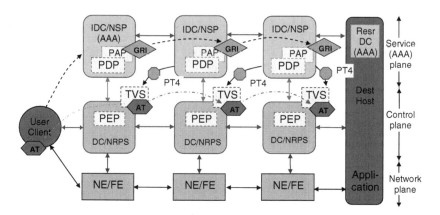

Fig. 1. Components involved in multidomain network resource provisioning. CRP stages reservation, deployment and access are presented by the flows correspondingly GRI (forward from the user to the resource), pilot tokens PT4 (backward), and access tokens AT (forward).

evaluates the request against the policy, and makes the decision whether to grant access or not.

Depending on the used authorisation and attribute management models, some attributes for the policy evaluation can be either provided in the request or collected by the PDP itself. It is essential in the Grid/Web services based service oriented environment that AuthN credentials or assertions are presented as a security context in the AuthZ decision request and are evaluated before sending request to PDP.

Based on a positive AuthZ decision (in one domain) the AuthZ ticket (Authz Ticket), containing AuthZ decision and context, can be generated by the PDP or PEP and communicated to the next domain where it can be processed as a security context for the policy evaluation in that domain.

In order to get access to the reserved resources (at the access stage) the requestor needs to present the reservation credentials that can be in a form of an AuthZ ticket (AuthzTicket) or an AuthZ token (AuthzToken) which will be evaluated by the PEP with support of TVS for ticket or token evaluation, to grant access to the reserved network elements or the resource. In more complex provisioning scenarios the TVS infrastructure can additionally support an interdomain trust management infrastructure for off-band token and token key distribution between domains that typically takes place at the deployment stage when access credentials or tokens are bound to the confirmed GRI by means of shared or dynamically created interdomain trust infrastructure. Token and token key generation and validation model can use either shared secret or PKI based trust model.

The TVS as a special GAAA-CRP component to support token-based signalling and policy enforcement mechanism is briefly described below.

It is an important convention for the consistent CRP operation that GRI is created at the beginning and sent to all polled/requested domains when running (advance) reservation process. Then in case of a confirmed reservation, the DC/NRPS will store the GRI and bind it to the committed resources. In addition, a domain can also associate internally the GRI with the Local Reservation Identifier (LRI). The proposed TVS and token management model allows for hierarchical and chained GRI-LRI generation and validation.

Correspondingly we define the following sessions in the overall CRP process: provisioning session that includes all stages; reservation session, and access session. All of them should share the same GRI and AuthZ context.

The proposed GAAA-CRP infrastructure includes the following access control mechanisms and components that extend the generic GAAA-AuthZ model described in [4] with the specific functionality for on-demand CRP, in particular:

- AuthZ session management to support complex AuthZ decision and multiple resources access, including multiple resources belonging to different administrative and security domains.
- AuthZ tickets with extended functionality to support AuthZ session management, delegation and obligated policy decisions.
- Access and pilot tokens used for interdomain reservation process management access control as part of the policy enforcement mechanisms that can be used in the control plane and in-band.
- Policy obligations to support usable/accountable resource access/usage and additionally global and local user account mapping widely used in Grid based applications and supercomputing.

The solutions proposed in the GAAA-CRP framework are based on using such structural components and solutions as the Token Validation Service, the Obligation Handling Reference Model (OHRM) [6], and the XACML attributes and policy profile for multidomain CRP that can combine earlier defined XACML-Grid and XACML-NRP profiles [7, 8].

3   Using Tickets and Tokens for Signalling and Access Control and Token Validation Service

In the proposed AuthZ architecture the tokens are used for access control and signalling at different CRP stages and considered as a flexible and powerful mechanism for communicating and signalling security context between domains. Tokens are abstract constructs/entities that refer to the related session context stored in the domains or by services. The GAAA-CRP uses three major types of the provisioning or AuthZ session credentials:

- AuthZ tickets that allow expressing and communicating the full/extended AuthZ session context and in this way could be used as access credentials.
- Access tokens that are used as AuthZ/access session credentials and refer to the stored reservation context.
- Pilot tokens that provide flexible functionality for managing the AuthZ session and the whole provisioning process.

Access tokens are used in rather traditional manner and described in details in [9]. Pilot token can be fully integrated into the existing network Control Plane interdomain protocols such as RSVP and GMPLS and in particular can be used as a container for AuthZ ticket in interdomain communication.

Although the tokens share a common data-model, they are different in the operational model and in the way they are generated and processed. The following elements and attributes are common for all tokens: GRI, DomainID, TokenID, TokenValue, - that allow unique token's identification and validation. More details about the token datamodel and processing can be found in the recent authors' paper [10].

In the proposed GAAA-CRP the token handling functionality is outsourced to the Token Validation Service (TVS) that supports different token handling models and store token and session related context.

Basic TVS functionality allows checking if a service/resource requesting subject or other entity, that possess current token, has permission to access/use a resource based on advance reservation to which this token refers. During its operation the TVS checks if a presented token has reference to a previously reserved resource and a request information conforms to a reservation conditions.

In a basic scenario, the TVS operates locally and checks a local reservation table directly or indirectly using a reservation ID (e.g. in a form of GRI). It is also suggested that in a multi-domain scenario each domain may maintain its Local Reservation ID (LRI) and provides its mapping to the GRI. In more advanced scenario the TVS should allow creation of a TVS infrastructure to support tokens and token related keys distribution to support dynamic resource, users or providers federations.

For the purpose of authenticating token origin, the pilot token value is calculated of the concatenated strings DomainId, GRI, and TokenId. This approach provides a simple protection mechanism against pilot token duplication in the framework of the same reservation/authorisation session.

The following expressions are used to calculate the TokenValue for the access token and pilot token:

```
TokenValue = HMAC(concat(DomainId, GRI, TokenId), TokenKey)
```

When using pilot tokens for signalling during interdomain resource reservation, TVS can combine token validation from the previous domain and generation of a new token with the local domain attributes and credentials.

4   Fine-Grained Policy Enforcement at Networking Layer

4.1   In-Band Policy Enforcement with TBN

The proposed GAAA-CRP architecture is easily integrated with the Token Based Networking (TBN) technology being developed at University of Amsterdam [11] to achieve in-band policy enforcement at dataflow layer. The TBN allows binding dataflows to users or applications by labeling application specific traffic, in particularly, our IPv4 implementation uses IPoption field to add a binary token to each IP packet. The token value is calculated similar to the XML token value by applying HMAC-SHA1 transformation to concatenated binary strings of the masked IP packet payload and GRI.

The TBN infrastructure consists of Token Based IP Switch (TBS-IP) that is controlled by inter-domain controllers in each domain. The TBS includes such major components as Token Builder (TB) and TVS that provides a similar functionality as defined in the GAAA-CRP framework. The applications' traffic is first tokenised by the *TB* of a local domain (e.g., a campus network), after which it is enforced by the *TBS-IP* at each domain along the end-to-end path.

Tokens are used to label dataflows and can be made independent of upper layer protocols. In this way the token can be regarded as an aggregation identifier to a network service. The following four types of aggregation identifiers that can be combined are defined:

- identifier to link a service to the NE (e.g., a multi-cast, or transcoding);
- identifier that defines the service consumer (e.g., the grid application);
- identifier that defines the serviced object (e.g., the network stream);
- identifier that defines the QoS (security, authorisation, deterministic property, etc.).

The semantics that is referred to by a token (e.g., a certain routing behaviour) can be hard-coded into a TBS or dynamically programmed via TVS. Hence, a token provides a generic way to match/link applications to their associated network services. Tokens can be either embedded in the application generated traffic or encapsulated in protocols where embedding is not supported, such as in public networks.

To provide necessary performance for multi-Gigabit networks, TBS-IP is implemented using Intel IXDP2850 network processor that has a number of built-in hardware cryptographic cores to perform basic cryptographic functions such as required for TBN operation HMAC, SHA1, digital signature and encryption [11, 12].

TBS-IP control plane relies on a master-slave communication using ForCES protocol described in details in the next section.

It is important to mention that the TBN functionality can support Multi-Level Security (MLS) model [13] by labelling and encrypting dataflows between security critical applications at data and control planes while GAAA-CRP model allows flexible policy based reservations and access control at service-plane.

4.2 Using ForCES for Network Management at Control and Data Planes

ForCES stands for Forwarding and Control Element Separation and is an upcoming IETF standard [14, 15]. ForCES defines a framework and associated protocol to standardize information exchange between the control and forwarding plane that comprise of Forwarding Elements (FE) and Control Elements (CE) correspondingly.

The basic building blocks of the ForCES model are the Logical Function Blocks (LFBs) described in an XML format. The ForCES protocol [15] works in a master-slave mode in which FEs are slaves and CEs are masters. The protocol includes commands for transport of LFB configuration information, association setup, status, and event notifications, etc. The protocol provides an open API for configuring and monitoring the Forwarding Plane in a standard manner. Grouping a number of LFBs, can create a higher layer service like TBS-IP in our case or a firewall. Similarly any security method at networking layer can be described using the ForCES model.

The ForCES standard framework defines the transport mapping layer (TML) to transfer the ForCES messages from the CE to the FE and vice versa. Currently defined is the SCTP TML that uses SCP protocol for secure messages exchange [16].

We consider the ForCES network management model as a way to integrate networking Control plane and Data plane into the general CRP process that requires heterogeneous networks configuration at least at the deployment and decommissioning stages. Recent works to define Web Services interfaces to ForCES devices makes such integration even simpler [17]. In our GAAA-CRP implementation we use ForCES protocol for transferring TBS-IP configuration information from the inter-domain controller to TB and TVS.

The ForCES framework provides a standard way of adding security services to both CE and FE. When used in the CRP/NRP Grid/Networking infrastructure the ForCES security framework [16] can benefit from using the common AuthN/AuthZ infrastructure. In this case the standard GAAA-AuthZ components can be added and related policies defined for the basic ForCES security functions such as endpoints and messages authentication.

5 GAAA-NRP Implementation in GAAA-TK Pluggable Library

All proposed GAAA-AuthZ functionality is currently being implemented in the GAAA Toolkit (GAAA-TK) pluggable Java library in the framework of the Phosphorus project [18]. The library provides also a basis for building AAA/AuthZ server that can act as Domain Central AuthZ Service (DCAS) or operates as a part of the Inter-Domain Controller (IDC) and allows for complex policy driven resource reservation and scheduling scenarios.

The library allows for AuthZ request evaluation with local XACML based PDP or calling out to the external DCAS using the SAML-XACML protocol. Current library implementation [19] supports both XACML-Grid and XACML-NRP policy and attribute profiles as configurable metadata set. For the convenience of application developers, the GAAA-TK provides simple XACML policy generation tools.

The TVS component is implemented as a part of the general GAAA-TK library but can also be used separately. It provides all required functionality to support token based policy enforcement mechanism that can be used at each networking layer and in particular for token based networking. All basic TVS functions are accessible and requested via a Java API. Current TVS implementation supports shared secret and PKI based token key distribution.

The GAAA TK library provides few PEP and TVS methods that support extended AuthZ session management and provide necessary AuthZ token and ticket handling functionality (refer to the GAAA-TK release documentation [20] for the complete API description). The two basic PEP methods provide simple AuthZ session management and allow using AuthZ tickets or access tokens as session credentials, however they differ in either requiring complete request information or using AuthZ ticket or token as only access credentials. Both of these methods can either return a valid AuthZ ticket or token, or "Deny" value.

6 Summary and Future Research

This paper presented the results of the ongoing research and development of the generic AAA AuthZ architecture in application to two inter-related research domains:

on-demand optical network resource provisioning and Grid based Collaborative Environment that can use the same Complex Resource Provisioning model.

The proposed AuthZ infrastructure will allow easy integration with the Grid middleware and applications what is ensured by using common Grid/network resource provisioning model that defines specific operational security models for the three major stages in the general resource provisioning: reservation, deployment or activation, and access or use. The current implementation of the GAAA-NRP authorisation infrastructure and GAAA-TK library in the Phosphorus project multidomain networking testbed provides a good basis for further research on improving efficiency of the provisioning and authorisation sessions management and extending functionality of the session management mechanisms such as discussed in this paper AuthZ tickets, access and pilot tokens.

The authors will continue research into developing security and trust models for the GAAA-CRP and CRP to define requirements for key management in multidomain environment. Currently proposed and implemented TVS infrastructure uses a shared secret security model that has known manageability problems.

The authors believe that the proposed solutions for AuthZ session management in on-demand resource provisioning will provide a good basis for further discussion among Grid and networking specialists.

Acknowledgements

This work is supported by the FP6 EU funded Integrated project PHOSPHORUS (Lambda User Controlled Infrastructure for European Research) IST-034115.)

References

1. Demchenko, Y., Wan, A., Cristea, M., de Laat, C.: Authorisation Infrastructure for On-Demand Network Resource Provisioning. In: Proceedings The 9th IEEE/ACM International Conference on Grid Computing (Grid 2008), Tsukuba, Japan, September 29 - October 1, pp. 95–103 (2008) IEEE Catalog Number CFP08GRI-CDR, ISBN 978-1-4244-2579-2
2. Hafid, A., Maach, A., Drissi, J.: A distributed advance reservation system for interconnected slotted optical networks: Design and simulations. Computer Communications 30(5), 1142–1151 (2007)
3. MSS Viola Meta Scheduling Service Project,
   http://packcs-e0.scai.fhg.de/viola-project/
4. Yuanming, C., Wendong, W., Xiangyang, G., Xirong, Q.: Initiator-Domain-Based SLA Negotiation for Inter-domain QoS-Service Provisioning. In: Proc. 4th Int. Networking and Services, March 16-21, pp. 165–169 (2008)
5. Vollbrecht, J., Calhoun, P., Farrell, S., Gommans, L., Gross, G., de Bruijn, B., de Laat, C., Holdrege, M., Spence, D.: AAA Authorization Framework. Informational RFC 2904, Internet Engineering Task Force (August 2000),
   ftp://ftp.isi.edu/in-notes/rfc2904.txt

6. Demchenko, Y., de Laat, C., Koeroo, O., Sagehaug, H.: Extending XACML Authorisation Model to Support Policy Obligations Handling in Distributed Applications. In: Proceedings of the 6th International Workshop on Middleware for Grid Computing (MGC 2008), Leuven, Belgium, December 1 (2008) ISBN:978-1-60558-365-5, http://portal.acm.org/citation.cfm?id=1462704.1462709

7. An XACML Attribute and Obligation Profile for Authorization Interoperability in Grids, Joint EGEE, OSG, and Globus document, https://edms.cern.ch/document/929867/1

8. Demchenko, Y., Cristea, C.M., de Laat: XACML Policy profile for multidomain Network Resource Provisioning and supporting Authorisation Infrastructure. In: IEEE International Symposium on Policies for Distributed Systems and Networks (POLICY 2009), London, UK, July 20-22 (2009) (accepted paper)

9. Gommans, L., Xu, L., Demchenko, Y., Wan, A., Cristea, M., Meijer, R., de Laat, C.: Multi-Domain Lightpath Authorization using Tokens. Future Generations Computer Systems 25(2), 153–160 (2009)

10. Demchenko, Y., de Laat, C., Denys, T., Toinard, C.: Authorisation Session Management in On-Demand Resource Provisioning in Collaborative Applications. In: COLSEC 2009 Workshop, The 2009 International Symposium on Collaborative Technologies and Systems (CTS 2009), Baltimore, Maryland, USA, May 18-22 (2009)

11. Cristea, M.-L., Gommans, L., Xu, L., Bos, H.: The Token Based Switch: Per-Packet Access Authorisation to Optical Shortcuts. In: Proceedings of IFIP Networking, Atlanta, GA, USA (May 2007)

12. ForCES Token Based Switch Design and Implementation, Phosphorus Project Deliverable D4.3.2 (September 30, 2008), http://www.ist-phosphorus.eu/files/deliverables/Phosphorus-deliverable-D4.3.2.pdf

13. Alkassar, A., Stuble, C.: Security Framework for Integrated Networks. In: Proc. Military Communications Conference (MILCOM 2003), October 13-16, vol. 2, pp. 802–807 (2003) ISBN: 0-7803-8140-8

14. Yang, L., Dantu, R., Anderson, T.: Forwarding and Control Element Separation (ForCES) Framework. RFC 3746 (April 2004)

15. Dong, L., Doria, A., Gopal, R.: ForCES Protocol Specification (work in progress) (March 2009), http://www.ietf.org/id/draft-ietf-forces-protocol-22.txt

16. Salim, J., Ogawa, K.: SCTP based TML (Transport Mapping Layer) for ForCES protocol (work in progress) (July 2009), http://www.ietf.org/internet-drafts/draft-ietf-forces-sctptml-04.txt

17. Haleplidis, E., Haas, R., Denazis, S., Koufopavlou, O.: A Web Service- and ForCES-based Programmable Router Architecture. In: IWAN 2005, France (2005)

18. Phosphorus Project, http://www.ist-phosphorus.eu/

19. GAAA Toolkit pluggable components and XACML policy profile for ONRP, Phosphorus Project Deliverable D4.3.1 (September 30, 2008), http://www.ist-phosphorus.eu/files/deliverables/Phosphorus-deliverable-D4.3.1.pdf

20. Updated GAAA Toolkit library for ONRP (final project release), Phosphorus Project Deliverable D4.5 (March 30, 2009), http://www.ist-phosphorus.eu/files/deliverables/Phosphorus-deliverable-D4.5.pdf

On the Definition of Access Control Requirements for Grid and Cloud Computing Systems

Antonios Gouglidis and Ioannis Mavridis

Department of Applied Informatics, University of Macedonia,
156 Egnatia Street, 54006, Thessaloniki, Greece
{agougl,mavridis}@uom.gr

Abstract. The emergence of grid and cloud computing systems has introduced new security concepts, so it requires new access control approaches. Traditional systems engineering processes can be enriched with helper approaches that can facilitate the definition of access control requirements in such complex environments. Looking towards a holistic approach on the definition of access control requirements, we propose a four-layer conceptual categorization. In addition, an example is given so that to demonstrate the utilization of the proposed categorization in a grid scenario for defining access control requirements, and evaluate their fulfilment vis-à-vis contemporary employed access control approaches.

Keywords: cloud computing, grid computing, access control, security requirements engineering.

1 Introduction

Grids [1] and clouds [2] are two promising computing technologies, which in the recent years have become the focal point of the science communities and the enterprises. However, contemporary implementations are characterised by an intrinsic complexity due to lack of standards, ad-hoc implementations and use of approaches which are not specifically designed for these environments. Access control is such an example. Security system designers need to define access control approaches that can cope with the complexity of these environments. Systems engineering can be used as a process in their development; however, an approach that incorporates the characteristics of these systems is non-existent. Therefore, we identify the need for a holistic approach in access control requirements definition that will enhance and facilitate the process of their identification and consequently, result in new access control models for grid and cloud computing environments.

Concerning access control approaches in current systems, we identify two main categories. The first is the Role-Based Access Control (RBAC) [3] and the second is the Usage Control (UCON) [4], [5]. The latter subsumes the Attribute Based Access Control approach (ABAC) [6]. To the best of our knowledge, there is no standard definition of ABAC [7] and for that we omit to further analyze it. RBAC supports the principles of abstract privileges, least privilege, separation of administrative functions

T. Doulamis et al.: (Eds.): GridNets 2009, LNICST 25, pp. 19–26, 2010.

and separation of duties [8]. Recent research in [9] has ventured to enhance RBAC to a next-generation access control approach by introducing the ASCAA principles. ASCAA stands for abstraction, separation, containment, automation and accountability. A grid authorization system that makes use of RBAC is PERMIS [10]. UCON has introduced a number of novelties such as rights that are determined during the access of an operation, mutability of attributes and decision continuity. More characteristics are the support of authorizations, obligations and conditions. Research has been done in [5] for its use in collaborative systems. UCON has been adopted in GridTrust [11]. However, as an attribute based approach, it inherits its complexity and can be error-prone, especially in highly heterogeneous environments [12].

The remainder of this paper is structured as follows: In section 2, a conceptual categorization for grid and cloud computing systems is proposed. A motivating scenario is presented in section 3, to demonstrate the identification of access control requirements based on the proposed categorization and assess their implementation in relation to contemporary approaches. Finally, the paper is concluded in section 4.

2   The Proposed Conceptual Categorization

Current grid systems have been categorized and classified in the existing literature based on different criteria, either qualitative or quantitative. Most of these categorizations are quite vague, in regard to the limits of each category [13]. This makes the definition of access control requirements a difficult process. Moreover, despite the use of generic systems engineering processes, security engineers lack a helper abstract model able to enhance and facilitate the definition of access control requirements. As a solution, a conceptual four-layer categorization that is capable of defining and evaluating security requirements is proposed.

Fig. 1. Conceptual categorization layers

As depicted in figure 1, the proposed conceptual categorization is based on four abstraction layers: entropy layer, assets layer, management layer and logic layer. The differentiation from generic security engineering approaches is that, in our case, factors that affect the security of the systems are mainly considered in their categorization. Briefly, the conceptual categorization identifies and groups security requirements into discrete layers of different abstraction levels. The abstraction level refers to the ability of a layer to identify requirements in different breadth and depth. The entropy layer identifies requirements from the dispersion of the objects in a system and the assets layer from the type of shared objects within the boundaries of the entropy layer. The next layer defines requirements from policy management and the logic layer incorporates requirements that are not handled by the former layers.

2.1 Entropy Layer

Entropy is a layer capable of capturing the abstract characteristics of a system accrued from its distribution. The term entropy refers to the virtual and geographic distribution of a system in association with the factor of time. Current classifications of grid systems are static and based mostly on the geographic distribution of their resources [14] or on their size [15]. The entropy layer uses existing grid distribution characteristics and the incorporated time factor in order to identify changes in the number of participating objects as well as alterations of them over time. Figure 2 depicts the entropy layer classification.

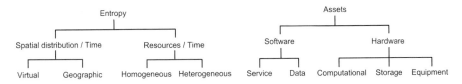

Fig. 2. Entropy layer classification   **Fig. 3.** Assets layer classification

In order to illustrate the flexibility of this layer in capturing the distribution characteristics of a system, we provide the examples of a volunteer desktop grid project named SETI@home [16] and of a science grid project named EGEE [17]. The data used to plot the graphs in figures 4 and 5 were taken from [18] and [19], respectively. The entropy lines represent the fluctuations in number of the involving objects, in relation to the spatial distribution over time. Issues like the authentication of the distributed objects can be examined under the entropy layer.

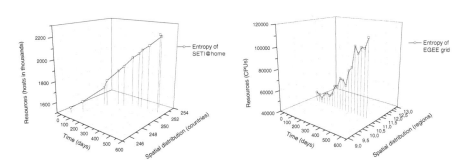

Fig. 4. Entropy of SETI@home   **Fig. 5.** Entropy of EGEE grid infrastructure

2.2 Assets Layer

The assets layer, as illustrated in figure 3, is used to wrap all the assets in a system. As an asset we define any sharable object in a system. In a grid system, an asset can either be of software or hardware type. The proposed classification in the assets layer is partially based on the existing literature [15], [20], and [21].

Under the software class, we further divide assets into two subclasses, these of service and data. Services have been used in the grid due to the adoption of service oriented architecture. The provision of fine-grained assets such as data is vital in a grid system. The requirement of sharing information at data-record-level in a database management system among a number of users is an illustrative example [22].

Similarly, we divide the hardware class into three distinct subclasses, those of computational, storage and equipment. Examples of computational assets are the usage of CPU or RAM of a system. Concerning the storage assets we mean the usage of raw storage space for the saving of data. Last but not least, an equipment is an asset that is usually used as an input or output device within a grid system.

2.3 Management Layer

The management layer is used to fulfil the need for capturing the security issues raised from the management of policies among the objects in a system as well as from trust relationships. Figure 6 illustrates the proposed classification.

The distribution level of a system, as defined in the entropy layer, affects the management of its policies. Usually, science grids with a high level of distribution require de-centralized management and vice-versa. Peer-to-peer networks are an example of de-centralized management, too. On the contrary, enterprise applications using cloud computing technologies require centralized management.

The enforcement of several management operations is another factor that needs to be further classified. Here, we identify two classification levels, that of static and dynamic enforcement. By static we refer to operations that can take place before and after the execution of a number of actions performed on an object by a subject. The dissimilarity between static and dynamic enforcement of operations is that, in the latter, the policy enforcement can also take place during the execution of an operation.

The automation level pertains exclusively to the intervention of an administrator to the management routines. Fully automation means that management is done by the system itself [23]. Semi automated systems are those that are partially managed by the system itself and the administrators. However, cases still exist where management automation is completely absent. Such systems are solely administered by humans. Operations, such as problem identification, conflict resolution and revocation of privileges should be considered under the management layer.

Finally, trust management must be taken under consideration in the process of security engineering. The life cycle of trust includes the creation, negotiation and management of it [24] and is considered to be an important part of security.

2.4 Logic Layer

The main concern of the logic layer is the application models and the type of their execution in a system. Based on the definition of grid and cloud computing systems and the requirements identified in the existing literature [13], [25], the classification of the logic layer as depicted in figure 7 is suggested.

The logic layer is split into two classes. The models class helps in the identification of security requirements that can rise from the nature of the application being executed in the grid. We propose a further classification of it into business and science applications. However, in both subclasses similar requirements exist. Usually the support of collaborations, workflows and co-operations fall under science projects. In addition, technologies such as infrastructure as a service (IaaS), platform as a service (PaaS) and software as a service (SaaS) are enterprise examples, which are usually met in cloud computing systems [2].

Furthermore, a classification of the execution mode of a grid or cloud application into batch and interactive can be made. Science projects usually require a batch-based execution of applications to provide results through the computation of data. In contrast, most business applications require an interactive environment to tackle the highly dynamic enterprise environment.

Fig. 6. Management layer classification   **Fig. 7.** Logic layer classification

3 Identifying Access Control Requirements

A generic grid access control scenario, enriched with some of cloud computing characteristics, follows. By applying our proposed conceptual categorization, we demonstrate the process of identifying access control requirements for the scenario.

The operational environment is illustrated in figure 8. The Virtual Organization (VO) is comprised of individually administered domains, which can dynamically join in or quit the collaboration. Users from the participating domains can request on demand usage of grid services. More precisely, the VO is comprised of companies A and B, represented respectively by domains A and B. An Application Service Provider (ASP) is a corporate organization that can share a number of pay-per-use services. A complementary entity provides a computational computing infrastructure (CCI). Users Alice from company A and Bob from company B require collaborating and producing a statistical analysis on a subset of their data. Figure 9 illustrates the information flow between the involving entities, on VO level. Users can request capabilities from their local domain, collaborate with other users, manage their data and request on demand the use of services. Services can be administered and also permitted to use segments of users' data via a delegation mechanism. In turn, a service can submit data segments to the CCI. Services can be provided as composite services, thus requiring automatically re-delegation mechanisms among the involving services. The system may prompt users for parameters completion during an operation, whose life span can vary, depending on the complexity of the computations. At the CCI, the resource owner can alter any access control policy for any resource and user at runtime. For instance, let's assume a policy that permits the execution of the statistical analysis application at the CCI for both Alice and Bob. However, prior to the statistical analysis completion, the resource owner restricts Bob's access with a new policy permitting him to use CPU cycles only when CCI is idle, thus leading to a delay of his computations, until the completion of Alice's job.

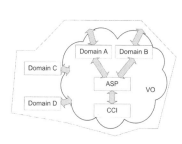

Fig. 8. Operational environment

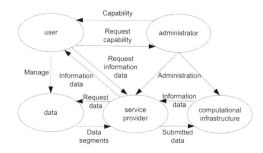

Fig. 9. Flow of information in a VO

Entropy requirements: The virtual distribution level of the system is low since there is only one formatted VO. On the other hand, the geographic distribution level that depends on the number of the participating domains can be high, which additionally entails heterogeneity issues. In order for the access control system to limit access to participating objects, it must be able to successfully authenticate them, since domains may make use of different authentication protocols. Furthermore, since the VO formation is not static, the access control system must continually observe all kinds of modifications.

As far as this scenario is concerned, UCON can cope with the complexity of the entropy layer. This is due to the support of attribute repositories that can be dispersed across the domains. The use of attributes also overcomes the heterogeneity issues. UCON is flexible enough to deal with the dynamic changes in the number of participants during the collaboration. On the contrary, RBAC handles better centralized architectures where participants are known a priori. Therefore, RBAC appears to be inappropriate for the current scenario and layer.

Assets requirements: Access control must be enforced on different types of assets. The scenario considers fine-grained access control on data, since it requires sending for computation only segments of users' data. The ASP provides a number of services and the CCI a number of hardware resources. Access control for both service and hardware level can be characterized as coarse-grained, since the scenario describes only permission, denial and restriction of access upon them. Thus, the access control model must be able to enforce fine-grained access control on data and coarse-grained on services and hardware resources, respectively.

UCON can handle fine-grained access control because of attributes. RBAC is rather coarse-grained compared to the former approach when it comes to assets definition. Assets, in RBAC, are grouped under roles and in order to become more granular, the assignments must be split into more. However, the use of context variables in known RBAC variations [26] overcomes such limitations. Once again, the UCON approach is preferred, since it supports natively fine-grained access control, and because it is easier to modify in order to support course-grained access control than for RBAC to support fine-grained access control.

Management requirements: In this scenario, a number of services uses segments of users' data and submits them at the CCI. This requires a delegation mechanism. Thus, the access control system must be able to support delegation of access rights from grid users to the ASP and CCI. A security issue is that of delegated rights revocation. We assume that delegated rights must be revoked after the completion of a job or on demand by the user. The former requirement demands from the access control system an automation level and the latter to apply changes dynamically. Furthermore, trust relationships must exist between the involving parties. In another use case, a user from an unknown domain may request to use a service. The access control system must be in position to decide whether to deny or provide limited access to the user. Policy conflict resolution must also be examined when composite services exist. This is required due to the inheritance of authorization rights amongst services.

Delegation of rights and trust relationships are supported by both access control approaches. Policy conflict resolution can be cumbersome for UCON, and easier for RBAC. In this case, a sensible choice would be the selection of RBAC, since it supports improved administrative capabilities compared to UCON. Revocation of user assignments, hierarchies and temporal constraints are some of RBAC's virtues making it superior in comparison to UCON.

Logic requirements: During Bob's collaboration with Alice, his access at the CCI has been restricted by the resource owner. This requires an access control system that must support dynamic collaborations. Occurring interactions between the user and the application require from the access control system to support them as well. More requirements are the support of stateful sessions due to long lived transactions and decomposition of composed services.

UCON is the only approach capable of supporting interactive environments via continuity of decisions and mutable attributes. Moreover, the use of obligations can handle well a number of business requirements. However, topics like service decomposition are left intact from all access control approaches.

4 Conclusions

Classic systems engineering processes have been used in the definition of access control requirements for grid and cloud computing systems. In many cases, this led to the adoption of existent or modified access control approaches. Furthermore, contemporary implementations seem to be inadequate in fulfilling the new security requirements set by these systems. Stemmed from the need to design new access control approaches and contemplating a helper holistic approach in defining security requirements, we recommended a four-layer conceptual categorization for grid and cloud computing systems. Its layered scheme is able to enhance and facilitate the process of defining access control requirements. We anticipate the proposed conceptual categorization to serve as a foundation in defining access control requirements and thus resulting in new access control models for grid and cloud computing systems.

References

1. Foster, I., Kesselman, C., Tuecke, S.: The anatomy of the grid - enabling scalable virtual organizations. International Journal of Supercomputer Applications 15 (2001)
2. Foster, I., Zhao, Y., Raicu, I., Lu, S.: Cloud computing and grid computing 360-degree compared. In: Grid Computing Environments Workshop, GCE 2008, pp. 1–10 (2008)

3. Ferraiolo, D.F., Sandhu, R., Gavrila, S., Kuhn, D.R., Chandramouli, R.: Proposed NIST standard for role-based access control. ACM Trans. Inf. Syst. Secur. 4(3), 224–274 (2001)

4. Sandhu, R., Park, J.: Usage control: A vision for next generation access control. Computer Network Security, 17–31 (2003)

5. Zhang, X., Nakae, M., Covington, M.J., Sandhu, R.: Toward a usage-based security framework for collaborative computing systems. ACM Trans. Inf. Syst. Secur. 11(1), 1–36 (2008)

6. Yuan, E., Tong, J.: Attributed Based Access Control (ABAC) for Web Services. In: Proceedings of the IEEE ICWS, pp. 561–569. IEEE Computer Society, Los Alamitos (2005)

7. Busch, S., Muschall, B., Pernul, G., Priebe, T.: Authrule: A generic rule-based authorization module, DBSec. Springer, Heidelberg (2006)

8. Sandhu, R.S., Coyne, E.J., Feinstein, H.L., Youman, C.E.: Role-based access control models. IEEE Computer 29(2), 38–47 (1996)

9. Sandhu, R., Bhamidipati, V.: The ASCAA principles for next-generation role-based access control. In: Availability, Reliability and Security, ARES 2008 (2008)

10. Chadwick, D.W., Otenko, A., Ball, E.: Role-based access control with X.509 attribute certificates. IEEE Internet Computing 7(2), 62–69 (2003)

11. GridTrust: Gridtrust (2009), http://www.gridtrust.eu/gridtrust

12. Priebe, T., Dobmeier, W., Kamprath, N.: Supporting attribute-based access control with ontologies. In: ARES 2006: Proceedings of the First International Conference on Availability, Reliability and Security, Washington, DC, USA, pp. 465–472. IEEE Computer Society, Los Alamitos (2006)

13. Alexander Kipp, S.W., Lutz Schubert, R.P., Horst Schwichtenberg, C.T., Karanastasis, E.: A new approach for classifying grids. Technical report, BEinGRID (2008)

14. Gridipedia: Types of grid (2009), http://www.gridipedia.eu/types-of-grids.html

15. Kurdi, H., Li, M., Al-Raweshidy, H.: A classification of emerging and traditional grid systems. IEEE Distributed Systems Online 9(3), 1 (2008)

16. SETI@home (2009), http://setiathome.ssl.berkeley.edu/

17. EGEE: Enabling grids for e-science, EGEE (2009), http://eu-egee.org/

18. BOINC: Boinc all projects statistics - distributed computing statistics (2009), http://www.allprojectstats.com/

19. Gridmap: Gridmap visualizing the "state" of the grid (2009), http://gridmap.cern.ch/gm

20. Green, D.: Grid technology. The future of the internet? The future of it (2002), https://ludit.kuleuven.be/nieuws/pdf/grid.pdf

21. Krauter, K., Buyya, R., Maheswaran, M.: A taxonomy and survey of grid resource management systems for distributed computing. Softw. Pract. Exper. 32(2), 135–164 (2002)

22. Broadfoot, P.J., Martin, A.P.: A critical survey of grid security requirements and technologies. Technical Report RR-03-15, Oxford University Computing Laboratory (2003)

23. Kephart, J.: Research challenges of autonomic computing. In: Software Engineering, ICSE 2005. Proceedings, pp. 15–22 (2005)

24. Chakrabarti, A.: Grid Computing Security, Managing Trust in the Grid. Springer, Heidelberg (2007)

25. Veit, D.J., Altmann, J. (eds.): GECON 2007. LNCS, vol. 4685. Springer, Heidelberg (2007)

26. Tolone, W., Ahn, G.J., Pai, T., Hong, S.P.: Access control in collaborative systems. ACM Comput. Surv. 37(1), 29–41 (2005)

Business Models, Accounting and Billing Concepts in Grid-Aware Networks

Serafim Kotrotsos[1], Peter Racz[2], Cristian Morariu[2], Katerina Iskioupi[1],
David Hausheer[2], and Burkhard Stiller[2]

[1] EXIS IT ltd, Vas.Sofias 98, GR-11528 Athens, Hellas
skotro@exis.com.gr
[2] Department of Informatics, University of Zurich
{racz,morariu,hausheer,stiller}@ifi.uzh.ch

Abstract. The emerging Grid Economy, shall set new challenges for the network. More and more literature underlines the significance of network - awareness for efficient and effective grid services. Following this path to Grid evolution, this paper identifies some key challenges in the areas of business modeling, accounting and billing and proposes an architecture that addresses them.

Keywords: Accounting, Billing, Model, Grid, Metering, Service, Network.

1 Introduction

Grid technology has emerged over the last few years as a new infrastructure concept which enables the sharing of computational and storage resources among multiple participants across administrative boundaries over the Internet. However, the current Internet is still largely based on its original design. This has been suitable for email and web applications that determined the major part of Internet traffic for many years, however, it has not been designed with large-scale Grid platforms in mind, which hit the limitations of the traditional Internet.

The EU-IST project EC-GIN [13] investigates how the network performance can be improved for Grid applications running on top of the Internet. One of the investigated scenarios in EC-GIN is the fast transfer of large files from one Grid node to another, key service for many grid applications. Under the assumption that between the two nodes there are multiple paths which do not share a common bottleneck, a large file transfer application may benefit from a higher throughput if transporting the file over multiple paths in parallel. In case that the network does not provide any support for source routing or multi-path routing, the only way to achieve a multi-path file transfer is by relaying the data transmission over different intermediate Grid nodes at the edge of the network.

However, a Grid node does only have an incentive to relay traffic if in return it gets some form of compensation which can either be monetary or non-monetary. Non-monetary incentive schemes are based on reciprocity, which uses barter-trade mechanisms [9], such as TFT [7] or PSH [1], can be used to provide incentives to nodes to

T. Doulamis et al.: (Eds.): GridNets 2009, LNICST 25, pp. 27–34, 2010.

relay services. However, if reciprocity cannot be assumed, due to the heterogeneity of a large-scale Grid system and the different needs of individual Grid users, monetary incentive schemes are required.

This paper proposes a traditional monetary-based incentive approach which follows a traditional accounting and billing architecture. The accounting keeps track of the amount of traffic relayed by each node in a row of relays between any source and destination and forwards that information to an accounting server. This data is used by the billing mechanism to be able to charge the users for the usage of those resources.

The key difference of the proposed accounting and billing architecture for Grid networks compared to other approaches is that it is based on a multi-domain approach supporting multiple virtual organizations and multiple network operators.

2 Large File Transfer Scenario

In the Large File Transfer (LFT) scenario several Grid operators cooperate in order to allow parallel use of existing network paths between two endpoints in the network. Since IP routing determines the best path to a certain destination, it is not possible to exploit several parallel paths by using IP routing mechanisms. Therefore, LFT uses Grid nodes as relays in order to route traffic from the sender to the receiver on multiple paths chosen by the sender.

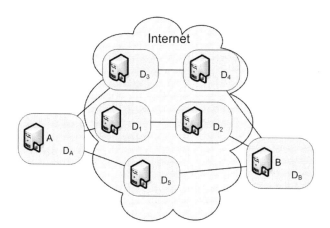

Fig. 1. Large File Transfer Scenario

Figure 1 depicts the LFT scenario, where node A in domain A (D_A) is the sender and node B in domain B (D_B) is the receiver. Due to multi-homing or peering agreements, there are several disjoint paths going through different domains between them. However, due to the way routing protocols work today, all packets sent by A to B will most probably follow the same path (the shortest in routing terminology). The use of an alternative path would only take place if the shortest path becomes unavailable. The use of parallel paths by routing algorithms in order to achieve load balancing is sometimes found within the network of an operator, but almost never on a larger scale, in multi-domain environments. Therefore, Grid nodes along the parallel paths have to act as relays forwarding data to the next hop.

In order to accurately keep track of the consumed resources on each node, appropriate accounting mechanisms need to be deployed. If the LFT transfer has to be paid for, a billing system is required besides accounting.

3 Business Models

Commercial cloud services as the ones released by Amazon in 2006 directly tap into the idea of utility computing [8]. The wide adoption of these services with pay-as-you-go schemes enable significant savings. Amazon Web Services have become already in 2008 the most successful "utility computing" realization. The 'Cloud' seems to be a business reality of the 'Grid' vision.

As clearly described in [12], the commercial use of Grid stimulates new business models, fitting the market demand of this new era. Moreover, in [11], the Grid economy is envisaged as a monetary model that will facilitate the sharing of resources between co-operating business partners.

In [2] and [3], a Grid business model and the term of computational economy framework are discussed. By adding grid - awareness to the equation, we come to a complete new picture of a new non-zero-sum market, where resource sharing and incentive - based economy increases productivity and efficiency for all parties.

A --> B	Resource Providers	Backbone Operators	Access Providers	Service Providers	Grid Operators	Content Providers	End Users
Resource Providers	X	X	V	X	V	X	X
Backbone Operators		V	V	X	X	X	X
Access Providers			X	V	X	X	V
Service Providers				V	V	V	V
Grid Operators					V	X	X
Content Providers						X	X
End Users							V

Fig. 2. A vision to Revenue sharing cases between Grid Economy parties

Up to cloud computing, business development has occurred only in the area of storage and computational resource sharing. This business is based on the traditional provider – consumer model. The addition of multi-path relay in the business shall dramatically alter this model, in a way similar the one Web 2.0 changed the content business! In the era of grid nodes providing multi-path relays, participating entities are constantly providers and consumers, the so called *prosumers*. Grid computing becomes an issue of many more organizations rather than cloud service providers.

The different types of business entities that are expected to play a role in the new business model are analyzed in the table of Figure 2. Checked cross-tabs illustrate an expected business relation. The revenue sharing agreements of the related entities define the requirements for the billing framework.

Having LFT scenario in mind, we analyze in the following paragraphs an architecture that materializes this vision into a usable infrastructure.

4 Architecture

Figure 3 depicts the overall Grid Economic architecture which includes besides the respective AAA and Billing components, a Pricing element that is responsible to determine the price for the service to be charged for, a Metering element that measures the amount of traffic forwarded by a node, and a Security element that maintains certificates for each relay node.

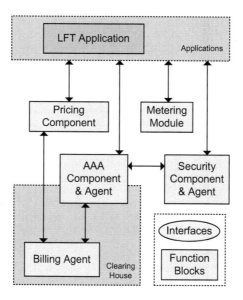

Fig. 3. Overall Grid Economics Architecture

4.1 Accounting

The accounting architecture is depicted in Figure 4. In order to assure interoperability, it is based on the IETF generic AAA (Authentication, Authorization, and Accounting) architecture [6]. The main components of the accounting architecture are the accounting server and the accounting client. Accounting servers (herein also referred as 'Clearing houses') consist of a distributed infrastructure responsible to collect accounting records from accounting clients and store them. Each operator domain has one or more accounting servers. The accounting client resides on the Grid node and it sends accounting records about resource usage and service consumption to the accounting server. The accounting client sends the accounting records to the server in its domain. Accounting data exchange between domains can only happen via the accounting servers. The accounting record transfer is based on the Diameter protocol [4]. Accounting records are routed to the corresponding accounting server (clearing house) based on the domain where the user is registered. Each server maintains a realm-based routing table that contains the next hop accounting server for each domain as well as a default route. The routing of accounting records fully complies with the Diameter routing specification [4] and allows multi-domain message routing.

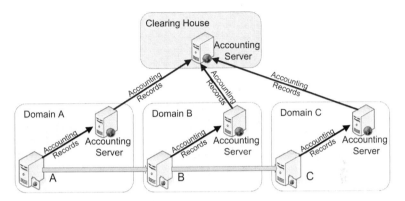

Fig. 4. Accounting Infrastructure

As Figure 4 shows, node A sends data to node C via node B. In order to enable billing across several domains, the accounting servers send accounting data to a clearing house. Clearing houses of our architectures are assumed as trusted organizations similar to the ones that clear up roaming charges among mobile telephony operators. They collect accounting records, compute service charges and bill end-users and domains. A clearing house's profit is derived by a commission on the transactions volume processed.

Each accounting record includes the origin and the destination of the record, the unique session identifier, the record number, a timestamp, the username, the identification of the data flow (src/dst addresses and ports), and usage statistics about the network usage (number of bytes and packets). The accounting records are transferred via the Diameter Accounting Request message and are acknowledged by the server via the Diameter Accounting Answer message.

4.2 Billing

The effort towards the realization of a realistic grid-aware network billing concept came across a key challenge: the goal to keep everything decentralized enabled the emerge of some conflicts of interest:

- A relay or a service domain might have reason to provide false accounting and / or billing data,
- A relay or a service domain might have reason to reduce quality or cancel service without documenting it,
- A client might question the service delivery or accounting / billing data collected by the relays and / or service domains.

For this reason we have introduced "clearing house" node hierarchy mentioned above. These nodes are considered as 3rd party trusted organizations that maintain balances for participating domains / hosts, host potential auction components of pricing, and correlate all accounting information in order to objectively clear-up transactions and balance updates, identify malicious behaviours and potentially set the penalties.

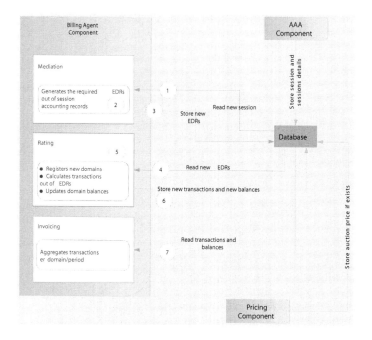

Fig. 5. Billing component structure and related interfaces

An additional design decision that has been made is that the client node considers that it receives the total service by the grid node that is price-wise or trust-wise selected. This node is considered as the total supplier for the session and encapsulates the cost and service of additional nodes, if it happens that the total supplier is actually a relay and not the end service node (service cascading). This assumption simplifies the rest of our analysis in defining the behaviour of the billing component between the client node and the supplier node.

The Billing component retrieves the respective information and executes the following operations in order to bill each service session: Mediation, Rating and Invoicing in a post-paid concept.

These operations refer to standard billing processes which have been here adjusted to the Grid Economy model and the LFT scenario.

Figure 5 depicts the design of the billing agent of the proposed architecture. The subcomponents included are:

Mediation: As soon as the AAA component stores completed session information in the database, the mediator reads it and creates a new Event Data Record (EDR).

Rating: The rating daemon is constantly polling the database in order to identify newly mediated EDRs and start processing them. Its functions include calculation of charges per EDR and updates of supplier/consumer balances.

Invoicing: The invoicing module is responsible for the aggregation of transaction information and the presentation of the results of the previous phases.

5 Architecture Advantages

In brief the proposed architecture is characterized by the following advantages:

- Support of accounting and charging across **multiple domains.**
- **Robustness** and scalability through the support of multiple parallel sessions to different accounting servers.
- **Security,** using IPSec and Transport Layer Security (TLS) over OpenDiameter library.
- **Simplicity** by applying *the* 'Service Cascading' concept and following the main structural blocks of state-of-the-art commercial billing infrastructures (mediation, rating, invoicing).
- **Flexibility,** since it does not limit the applicability in a specific pricing / discounting policy, services, business relationships or network infrastructure.
- **Feasibility**, since no complex pricing algorithms or metrics have been used however all complexity that the business relations are expected to have is supported.
- **Trust,** due to the existence of clearing house entities among the business parties, an approach pragmatic in network economies as the one of wireless telephony.

6 Conclusions

The business models, accounting and billing techniques analyzed in this paper provide a framework for realistic incentive - based networks that provide explicit support for grid applications. The experiments conducted so far with the generic problem of Large File Transfer service have verified that this architecture is scalable, efficient and feasible over the standard internet, with limited implications. Further experiments and evaluations are in progress with an immediate goal the integration and evaluation of this architecture with real-time streaming services (e.g. VoD, IPTV) provided by multiple different alternative hosts / domains.

Acknowledgements

This work has been performed partially in the framework of the EU IST project EC-GIN under the contract STREP FP6-2006-IST-045256. Additionally, the authors would like to acknowledge discussions with all of their colleagues and project [13] partners.

References

1. Bocek, T., Kun, W., Hecht, F.V., Hausheer, D., Stiller, B.: PSH: A Private and Shared History-based Incentive Mechanism. In: Hausheer, D., Schönwälder, J. (eds.) AIMS 2008. LNCS, vol. 5127, pp. 15–27. Springer, Heidelberg (2008)
2. Buyya, R., Stockingerz, H., Giddy, J., Abramson, D.: Abramson: Economic Models for Management of Resources in Grid Computing (2001)
3. Buyya, R., Abramson, D., Giddy, J.: A Case for Economy Grid Architecture for Service Oriented Grid Computing. In: 15th International Parallel and Distributed Processing Symposium, pp. 776–790 (2001)
4. Calhoun, P., Loughney, J., Guttman, E., Zorn, G., Arkko, J.: Diameter Base Protocol. IETF RFC 3588 (September 2003)
5. Hausheer, D., Stiller, B. (eds.): Implementation of Economic Grid Traffic Management and Security Mechanisms. Deliverable D4.1 of the EC-GIN Project (May 2009)
6. de Laat, C., Gross, G., Gommans, L., Vollbrecht, J., Spence, D.: Generic AAA Architecture. IETF RFC 2903 (August 2000)
7. Lian, Q., Peng, Y., Yang, M., Zhang, Z., Dai, Y., Li, X.: Robust Incentives via Multi-level Tit-for-tat. In: 5th International Workshop on Peer-to-Peer Systems (IPTPS 2006), Santa Barbara, CA, USA (February 2006)
8. LaMonica, M.: Amazon: Utility computing power broker, CNET News.com (November 2006), http://news.cnet.com/2100-7345_3-6135977.html
9. Obreiter, P., Nimis, J.: A Taxonomy of Incentive Patterns - The Design Space of Incentives for Cooperation. In: Moro, G., Sartori, C., Singh, M.P. (eds.) AP2PC 2003. LNCS (LNAI), vol. 2872, pp. 89–100. Springer, Heidelberg (2004)
10. Stiller, B., Hausheer, D. (eds.): Design of Economic Grid Traffic Management and Security Mechanisms. Deliverable D4.0 of the EC-GIN Project (May 2008)
11. Weishaupl, T.: Business and the Grid, Economic and Transparent Utilization of Virtual Resources; Dissertation, Universitaet Wien (October 2005)
12. IST Workshop: Grid Economy and Business Models; part of 2003 Grid related Conference in Milan, titled Harnessing computing and knowledge resources, http://cordis.europa.eu/ist/grids/grid_economy_and_business_models.htm (accessed: 04 September 2007)
13. The EC-GIN Consortium: Europe-China Grid InterNetworking (EC-GIN), Specific Targeted Research Project (STREP), http://www.ec-gin.eu/ (last access June 2009)

Part II

General Session 2

Network Centered Multiple Resource Scheduling in e-Science Applications

Yan Li, Sanjay Ranka, Sartaj Sahni, and Mark Schmalz

Department of Computer and Information Science and Engineering
University of Florida, Gainesville, Florida 32611
{yanli,ranka,sahni,mssz}@cise.ufl.edu

Abstract. Workflows generated from e-Science applications require the simultaneous use of multiple types of resources. In this paper, we present the Multiple Resource Reservation Model ($MRRM$), which enables the monitoring and scheduling of multiple heterogeneous and distributed resources. $MRRM$ provides a unified representation for multiple types of distributed resources, and represents resource constrains such as compatibility and accessibility. Using $MRRM$, we solve the Multiple Resource First Slot problem based on a collection of algorithms that are customized for different request and resource types. Our simulation results demonstrate efficiency and scalability of our algorithms for various sizes of networks and resource sets.

1 Introduction

Many e-Science applications require the simultaneous use of multiple types of resources. To fulfill such multiple resources requirements, we propose a framework for conducting admission control and in-advance reservations on various computational resources such as network bandwidth, CPU, storage and even software licenses.

Resource Reservation has been long studied as an important approach to provide QoS guarantee. In the network field, bandwidth reservation is the major concern. Either **on-demand scheduling** or **in-advance scheduling** has been characterized by a set of algorithms and systems [1, 2, 3, 4, 5]. On the other hand, in system and architecture field, many paper also focused on CPU of storage resources reservation. [6, 7, 8]. For example, Maui [8], which is a popular high-performance computing scheduler for clusters and supercomputers, do not schedule network resources, although they are able to do advance reservation of resources such as CPU and storage. On the other hand, network bandwidth management systems such as those for UltraScienceNet (USN) and ESnet do not schedule computer resources. The Sharc system [7] modeled both network and CPU resources in the clusters as unified resources blocks, but the constrains among resources, such as network topology, resource compatibilities are not considered.

In this paper, we envisioned those large scale e-Science applications which consist of dedicated networks with hundreds of nodes, and computational resources

T. Doulamis et al.: (Eds.): GridNets 2009, LNICST 25, pp. 37–44, 2010.

with different platforms. When multiple resources are reserved, their topologies, dependencies, and compatibilities must be handled. The purpose of our paper is to develop a co-scheduler that simultaneously schedules multiple types of resources with a network focus based on a our Multiple Resources Reservation Model ($MRRM$). We also solved a Multiple Resource First Slot problem ($MRFS$) with the objective of determining the earliest time that can be used to reserve all resources required to compute a given request.

The rest of the paper is organized as follows. In Section 2 we give the detail of our resource model $MRRM$ and define the related data structures. In Section 3 we introduce the $MRFS$ problem and formally define the request pattern. In Section 4, we propose our algorithms for multi-resource scheduling. In Section 5, we evaluate these algorithms to show their effectiveness. The conclusions are drawn in Section 6.

2   Resource Model and Data Structure

2.1   Resource Model: $MRRM$

In this paper, the Multiple Resources Reservation Model ($MRRM$) is defined to provide a unified presentation for different types of resources. In e-Science applications, resources can be classified into network resources and local computational resources. Network resources, including links, routers and switches, transfer user's data from one site to another. Local computational resources include CPU, storage and other resources that are used in processing user requests. $MRRM$ is modeled as a graph $G < V, E >$ with the communication network in the middle, and computational resources attached to network edge nodes. Each switch or router is represented as a node in V, while each network link is mapped to an edge in E. The local computational resources attached to one of the edge routers. A single resource unit is modeled as an edge in that subgraph.

As the resources maybe of different types, we assign each resource link a type ID ($T - ID$), to specify its type - for example, CPU, Memory. With the type ID, all local resources can be grouped into one of several multi-partitioned resource constraint graphs (MPRCGs), which is presented in Figure 1. Three resource partitions are presented:Resource A, B and C. However, $T - ID$ is not enough, as the resources with same type(CPU) may not be cooperate together(X86 and MIPS). So we also provide a compatibility ID (C-ID) to each resource. $C - ID$ facilitates grouping of resources with the same T-ID into smaller groups of compatibility, as shown in the smaller grey cycles in partition A and C in Figure 1. With both $T - ID$ and $C - ID$, user's preference on various resources can be explicitly specified.

A further consideration involves accessibility. For example, some computers use Distributed Shared Memory to provide all CPU nodes full access to the memory model. However, other systems only allow certain CPUs to access specific memory partitions. Our MRRM is capable of handling both scenarios. If two resource links within different MPRCGs are accessible to each other, then a specific auxiliary link with unlimited capacity connects the two links. The connections

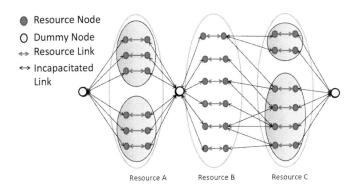

- ● Resource Node
- ○ Dummy Node
- ↔ Resource Link
- ↔ Incapacitated Link

Resource A   Resource B   Resource C

Fig. 1. Detailed Model of MRRM

between partition B and C in Figure 1 give an example of such scenarios. If all resources in one MPRCG are accessible to all resources in another MPRCG, then a connection is made at the MPRCG level, so that every resource link in either MPRCG is connected with every resource link in the other MPRCG, as shown in Figure 1 between partition A and B.

2.2 Data Structures

In $MRRM$, the status of each resource unit is maintained using a Time-Resource list (TR list). It is comprised of tuples of the form (t_i, r_i), where t_i is a time and r_i is the amount of resources. The tuples on a TR list are in increasing order of t_i. If (t_i, r_i) is a tuple of $TR[l]$ (other than the last one), then the amount of available resource l from t_i to t_{i+1} is r_i. When (t_i, r_i) is the last tuple, there are r_i units of resource l available from t_i to ∞.

We also employ two other data structures: ST(Start Time) List and Basic Interval. ST List, like TR List, is also associated with a resource link and is directed computed from the corresponding TR list and current request. First, we define, for each edge (u, v), an ST list $ST(u, v)$, which is comprised of pairs of the form (a, b), $a \leq b$. The pair (a, b) has the below interpretation: for every start time $x \in [a, b]$, edge (u, v) has enough resources from time x to time $x + dur$ to fulfill the current request. As proved in [5], The earliest start time is the smallest a_i for which there is an path p from s to d in the graph and every edge in p has a ST interval contains this a_i.

Basic Interval is a time interval $[t_i, t_{i+1}]$, where $t_i < t_{i+1}$ and within a Basic Interval, for any edge $e \in E$ in our multi-resource graph, its status, like bandwidth or disk spaces, remains static. Also, any two disjoint steady stages are independent from each other: any change on the link status in one Basic Interval will not affect the scheduling result in any other steady stages. To build a list that contain all the Basic Intervals, we first consider the time part of a edge's TR list, $t_0, t_1, t_2...t_q$, any time interval $[t_i, t_{i+1}]$ forms a steady stage of that link. Hence, if we union the time parts of each resource link's TR list together, we will obtain a list for all Basic Intervals.

3   Problem Definition

In **MRFS** scenario, the user's request to have the job starts as early as possible within a specific time window. If the request is feasible at some time within the reservation window, the earliest time t will be reported to the user and the corresponding resources will be reserved, or else, the request will be rejected.

A $MRFS$ request is a 6-tuple (s, d, dur, $ResWin < st, et >$, $RV < R_0, R_1, R_2... >$, $shareable$). s and d are the source and destination node of the data transfer, the computational resources attached to s and d are the computational resources that are going to be reserved. dur is the duration that those resources needs to be reserved. $ResWin < st, et >$ is the reservation window, which means the job's start time must be in the time interval $[st, et - dur]$. RV is a vector that contains the all resource requirements. $shareable$ flag specifies whether the job can be split among different resource units.

4   Multiple Resource Scheduling Algorithm

Based on whether job can be split and whether the local resources are fully accessible(i.e. resources in one layer can access part of the resources in its neighborhood layer or all of them), we divided the MRFS problem into 4 sub-problems:

WS-RC: The workload can be split, and local computational resources are constrained on accessibility.

WN-RC: The workload cannot be split, but local computational resources are constrained on accessibility.

WS-RN: The workload can be split, and local computational resources are not constrained on accessibility.

WN-RN: The workload cannot be split, but local computational resources are not constrained on accessibility.

4.1 $WS - RC$ Scheduling Algorithm

If the workload can be split, then given request r_i and the multi-resource graph G, our $WS - RC$ algorithm discovers the maximum flow from source's sink to destination's sink for each basic interval within the reservation window. The scheduler then attempts to identify (a) if there are enough resources within the current basic interval BI_i, if true, BI_i is marked as feasible; and (b) whether or not there exists one consecutive (i.e., temporally connected) sequences of basic intervals $[BI_i, BI_{i+1}, ..., BI_j]$ with total length longer than the required duration dur. If such a sequence is found, then the earliest possible start time of the sequence becomes the first possible start time of the user's request. The detail of $WS - RC$ Scheduling Algorithm is shown in the left part of Figure 2.

To apply the traditional max-flow algorithm to the various times of resources, we need the scale the capacity of different types of resource links to one Base

WS-RC Scheduling (req $_i$, G) {

  Randomly choose resource r_k as base resource;

  G' = Scale(G, r_k);

  Build the global time list L from G', remove all the T_i
      outside the scheduling window req$_i$.ResWin;

  Identify all the Steady Stages;

  For each Steady Stage SS$_i$ {

    MF$_i$ = MaxFlow(G', SSi);

    if(MF$_i$ ≥ basevalue)

    Mark SS$_i$ as a feasible Steady Stage;

  }

  Traverse the Steady Stage list again. find out the
      first consecutive feasible steady stages list which
      is longer than req$_i$.dur;

  if (such list exist);

    accept the request;

    set list's the start time as request's start time;

  else

    reject the request;

}

Extended Bellman-Ford (s,d) {

  initialize st(*) = st(0, *);

  // compute st(*) = st(n − 1, *)

  put the source vertex into list1;

  for (int k = 1; k < n; k++) {

    // see if there are vertices

    whose st value has changed

    if (list1 is empty)

      break; // no such vertex

    while (list1 is not empty) {

      delete a vertex v from list1;

    for (each edge (v, u)) {

      st(u) = st(u) ∪ {st(v) ∩ ST (v, u)};

      if (st(u) has changed and

      u is not on list2)

        add u to list2;

    }

    list1 = list2; make list2 empty;

}}}

Fig. 2. Algorithms for $WS - RC$(left) and $WN - RC$(right)

Value or the flow that is directly computed will not make any sense. Here, we chose network bandwidth as our base resource. If bandwidth's request be $10(MB/s)$ and CPU's request be $5(GHz)$, we scale all the CPU resource links' capacity by a factor of 2 and we also need to set the CPU to requirement from $5GHz$ to $10GHz$. In this way, we achieve the numeric unification among different type of resources in $MRRM$, which enables the min-cut algorithm [9] to be applied directly on our scaled graph.

The complexity of the above $WS - RC$ scheduling algorithm is $O(|SS_{RW}| * N^3)$, where $|SS_{RW}|$ is the size of Basic Interval list what is within the reservation window and $N = N_N + N_s + N_d$. N_N is the number of nodes in the network. N_s and N_d the number of local computational resources attached to s and d.

4.2 $WN - RC$ Scheduling Algorithm

In the $WN - RC$ case, the workload can only be transferred on a single path in the network and can only be processed using a single unit of each type local computational resources. So we use the Extended Bellman-Ford algorithm [5] to solve this problem. The algorithm is presented in the right part of Figure 2.

First, we will extend the concept of an ST list for an edge a path. Let $st(k, u)$ be the union of the ST lists for all paths from vertex s to vertex u that have at most k edges on them. Clearly, $st(0, u) = \emptyset$ for $u \neq s$ and we assume $st(0, s) =$

$[0, \infty]$. Also, $st(1, u) = ST(s, u)$ for $u \neq s$ and $st(1, s) = st(0, s)$. For $k > 1$ (actually also for $k = 1$), we obtain the following recurrence

$$st(k, u) = st(k - 1, u) \cup \{\cup_{v:(v,u) \text{ is an edge}}$$
$$\{st(k - 1, v) \cap ST(v, u)\}\} \qquad (1)$$

where $\cup$ and $\cap$ are list union and intersection operations. For an n-vertex graph, $st(n - 1, d)$ gives the start times of all feasible paths from s to d. The Bellman-Ford algorithm [10] may be extended to compute $st(n - 1, d)$.

It is easy to see that the computation of the $st(*, *)$s may be done in place (i.e., $st(k, u)$ overwriting $st(k-1, u)$) and the computation of the sts terminated when $st(k - 1, u) = st(k, u)$ for all u. With the above observation, here we give the detail of Extended Bellman-Ford algorithm.

Each iteration of the **for** loop takes $O(L)$ time, where L is the length of the longest st list. Since this **for** loop is iterated a total of $O(N * E)$ times, the complexity of the extended Bellman-Ford algorithm is $O(N * E * L)$, where N and E is the number of nodes and links in the whole multiple resource graph.

When using the extended Bellman-Ford algorithm to solve the first slot problem, we first find the earliest start time t for a feasible path using Extended Bellman Ford algorithm. Then, the actual path may be computed using BFS where the feasibility of each link is computed by fixed the job's $t_{start} = t$ and $t_{end} = t + dur$. Also BFS guaranteed to find the shortest feasible path in the graph.

4.3 $WS - RN$ Scheduling Algorithm

In the $WS - RN$ scenario, although the $WS - RC$ scheduling algorithm can directly be applied, there still exists a much fast algorithm: First, we compute the available ST List in network from the source edge router to the destination edge router, using the $WS - RC$ algorithm. Second, we compute the available time slots for local resources by checking, for each computational resource partition at source and destination, whether any set of compatible resources can provide sufficient resources to satisfy the user's job request. Given a certain partition in a MPRCG, we group all the compatible resources together, and compute the aggregate TR list for this compatibility group. Then, we compute the ST list according to current request and union all the group ST List to produce a ST list for the current partitions. Finally, we intersect the network's ST list with the ST lists specific to all local resource partitions, to determine availability of a start time.

In this algorithm, we only check each local resource stage for each corresponding request by visiting each resource link for $O(1)$ times. Since the list union and intersection can also be finished in linear time, we can reduce the algorithm run time to $O(|SS_{RW}| * (N_s + N_N^3 + N_d))$.

4.4 $WN - RN$ Scheduling Algorithm

The $WN - RN$ problem is similar to the previous $WS - RN$ problem. In particular, a network path can be computed via the *Extended Bellman-Ford* algorithm to yield the first start time. This computation is followed by *breadth-first search* to identify the path. For local computational resources, we can apply the same approach as in $WS - RN$. However, $WN - RN$ neglects the grouping of resources according to compatibility. Since the requested job cannot be split, only one resource unit in each resource partition is required. In that case, the algorithm's complexity is bounded by $O(N_N * E_N * L + N_s + N_d)$

5   Evaluation

We tested our work on a USNET simulator at Oak Ridge National Laboratory (ORNL). The evaluation results are presented below.

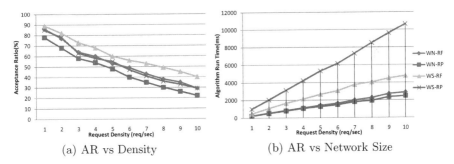

(a) AR vs Density   (b) AR vs Network Size

Fig. 3. Acceptance ratio changing with (a)request density; (b)network size.

Figures 3a Figures 3b provides the average acceptance ratio and algorithm run time as a function of request density, respectively. The result is acquired using a 100 node random network with 15 randomly selected local resources sites.

Our experiment results show the following:

1. The increase of request density will degrade every algorithms' performance. As more request come into the system within the same time interval, the network and clusters becomes congested, hence more requests were rejected since not enough resources are available. In the mean time, as more requests are running in the system simultaneously, the length of Basic Interval list and ST list increases, which leads to longer algorithms' run time.
2. When multiple paths are allowed and resources are fully shared, the scheduler can better utilize system resources, so as to accept more requests. However, the resulting multi-path algorithms require more computation time to obtain a feasible result.
3. Generally speaking, all 4 algorithms scales very well with either system size or request density. Even when the workload is high, one request averagely takes less than a minute to find out scheduling result.

6   Conclusion

In this paper, we consider the multiple resource scheduling problem, and present several solutions in terms of a multi-resource model. In e-Science, computational resources are widely distributed and are connected by fast optical networks. Thus, we propose a co-scheduling solution comprised of a flexible and efficient multi-resource reservation model ($MRRM$) and solve four instances of the multiple reservation first slot ($MFRS$) problem. Based on our model, four algorithms were developed to solve salient instances of $MRFS$. Experiments on a heterogeneous computer network showed that our algorithms are scalable linearly in terms of network size and request ratio.

Acknowledgement

This work was supported, in part, by the National Science Foundation under grant 0312038 and 0622423. Any findings, conclusions or recommendations expressed in this material are those of the authors and do not necessarily reflect the views of NSF. The work was also supported in part by a grant from UltraHiNet and Florida High Tech Corridor.

References

1. Aukia, P., Kodialam, M., Koppol, P.V.N., Lakshman, T.V., Sarin, H., Suter, B.: RATES: A server for MPLS traffic engineering. IEEE Network, 34–41 (March/April 2000)
2. Guerin, R., Orda, A., Williams, D.: Qos routing mechanisms and ospf extensions. IETF Internet Draft (1996)
3. On-demand secure circuits and advance reservation system, http://www.es.net/oscars
4. Guerin, R.A., Orda, A.: Qos routing in networks witrh inaccurate information: Theory and algorithms. IEEE/ACM Transactions on Networking 7(3), 350–364 (1999)
5. Sahni, S., Rao, N., Ranka, S., Li, Y., Jung, E.S., Kamath, N.: Bandwidth scheduling and path computation algorithms for connection-oriented networks. In: Sixth International Conference on Networking (ICN 2007), p. 47 (2007)
6. Urgaonkar, B., Pacifici, G., Shenoy, P., Spreitzer, M., Tantawi, A.: An analytical model for multi-tier internet services and its applications. In: Proc. of ACM SIGMETRICS, pp. 291–302 (2005)
7. Urgaonkar, B., Shenoy, P.: Sharc: Managing cpu and network bandwidth in shared clusters. Technical report, IEEE Transactions on Parallel and Distributed Systems (2001)
8. Maui, http://www.clusterresources.com/pages/products/maui-cluster-scheduler.php/
9. Ahuja, R., Magnanti, T., Orin, J.: Network Flows: Theory, Algorithms, and Applications. Prentice-Hall, Englewood Cliffs (1993)
10. Sahni, S.: Data structures, algorithms, and applications in C++, 2nd edn. Silicon Press (2005)

Percolation-Based Replica Discovery in Peer-to-Peer Grid Infrastructures

Francesco Palmieri

Federico II University of Napoli,
Via Cinthia, 5, Complesso Universitario di Monte S. Angelo, 80126 Napoli, Italy
`francesco.palmieri@unina.it`

Abstract. Peer-to-peer Grids are collaborative distributed computing/data processing systems, characterized by large scale, heterogeneity, lack of central control, unreliable components and frequent dynamic changes in both topology and configuration. In such systems, it is desirable to maintain and make widely accessible timely and up-to-date information about shared resources available to the active participants. Accordingly we introduce a scalable searching framework for locating and retrieving dataset replica information in random unstructured peer-to-peer Grids built on the Internet, based on a widely known uniform caching and searching algorithm. Such algorithm is based on bond percolation, a mathematical phase transition model well suited for random walk searches in random power law networks, which automatically shields low connectivity nodes from traffic and reduces total traffic to scale sub-linearly with network size. The proposed schema is able to find the requested information reliably end efficiently, even if every node in the network starts with a unique different set of contents as a shared resources.

Keywords: P2P Grids, content search, percolation.

1 Introduction

Grid is an exciting buzzword in the computing world today, mainly in the scientific area. It is usually defined as the exploitation of a varied set of networked computing resources, including large or small computers, storage/file servers and special purpose devices. The emerging Internet based peer-to-peer (P2P) Grid infrastructures, which are based on a "flat" organization allowing seamless discovery, access to, and interactions among resources and services, have complex and highly dynamic computational and interaction behaviors resulting in significant development and management challenges. P2P Grid infrastructures have the potential of a disruptive technology since they can aggregate enormous storage and processing resources while minimizing the overall costs and greatly reducing or avoiding at all the need for centralized servers. A P2P assembly of general purpose nodes connected through the Internet can evolve better from small configurations to larger ones, ensuring almost unlimited scalability features. In such totally distributed architecture, we increasingly face the problem of providing to the running applications fast and reliable access to large data volumes, often stored into datasets geographically distributed across the network. As a direct

T. Doulamis et al.: (Eds.): GridNets 2009, LNICST 25, pp. 45–56, 2010.

consequence, the concept of replication, that is the distribution of multiple copies of a data source of interest across multiple grid nodes, to be processed locally when needed, has been adopted by grid community to increase data availability and maximize job throughput. Replication starts with an initial data discovery operation aiming to detect all the copies of the required dataset already existing on the Grid, given its logical file name. In traditional grids a centralized catalogue is searched in order to find all the locations where the requested dataset is available, obtaining a list of all the already available replicas. A dataset itself can consist of several physical files but the end-user normally only knows the dataset concept. Unfortunately, the peer to peer paradigm by definition, excludes any form of centralized structure, requiring resource management and control to be completely decentralized, hence no traditional catalog service o centralized search facility can be implemented in P2P grids. In such systems, it is however desirable to maintain and make widely accessible timely and up-to-date information about active participants such as services offered and replicated dataset resources available. It is not obvious how to enable powerful discovery query support and collective collaborative functionality that operate on such a distributed and unstructured organization as a whole, rather than on a given part of it. Further, it is not obvious how to allow for the propagation of search results that are fresh, allowing time-sensitive dynamic content. To cope with the above challenges, we introduce a scalable searching framework for locating and retrieving shared replica information in random unstructured peer-to-peer Grids built on transport networks, such as the Internet, characterized by Power-Law, scale-free network structure and heavy-tailed degree distributions. Such framework is based on a known searching and local uniform caching algorithm based on bond percolation, a mathematical phase transition model well suited for random walk searches in random power law networks, which automatically shields low connectivity nodes from traffic and reduces total traffic to scale sub-linearly with network size. Our focus here is on the adaptability of the search network, dynamically accommodating changes in the data and query distribution, when nodes and data are continually joining and leaving the P2P system. Unlike other P2P information retrieval solutions, there is no need to assume that multiple copies of the shared information made available must be present on the Grid; the proposed schema is able to find the requested information reliably end efficiently, even if every node in the network starts with a unique different set of or objects.

2 Related Work

Several papers have analyzed search strategies for unstructured decentralized P2P infrastructures. Some of these strategies have been also used to implement search facilities in P2P grids [1]. Content-based search techniques include content-mapping networks [2][3][4]. In such schemes, when a peer joins a network it is assigned a responsibility to index a "zone" of the advertisement space in such a way that the union of the indices of all the peers covers the whole advertisement space. The paper in [5] explores alternatives (expanding rings and random walks) to the classical flooding search strategies whereas [6] exploits the theory of random graphs to prove properties of a generalization of the search that combines flooding and random walks. The work in [7] focuses on random walks and introduces a number of local search strategies that utilize high degree nodes in power-law graphs to reduce search time. The work in [8] quantifies the effectiveness of random walks for searching and construction of unstructured P2P networks. It also compares flooding and random walk by simulations on different network topologies. On the other side, [9] introduces a scalable searching approach for locating contents in random networks with heavy-tailed degree distributions. The analysis of the size of the giant connected component of a random graph with heavy tailed degree distributions under bond percolation is the heart of their results on which also our scheme is based.

3 P2P Grid Infrastructures

The traditional early production grid architectures are based on a service-oriented computing model with a super-local resource management and scheduling strategy. In detail, the overall control logic is based on a certain number of centralized managers that are the only entities with a complete view of the resources available on the whole Grid or on their own local management domain. On the other side, the P2P model, that has achieved wide prominence in the context of multimedia file exchange, allows the distributed computing concept to reach out to harness the outer edges of the Internet and consequently will involve scales that were previously unimaginable. The client/server architecture does not exist in a peer-to-peer system. Instead, peer nodes act as both clients and servers - their roles are determined by the characteristics of the tasks and the status of the system. Conceptually, these new computing infrastructures are characterized by decentralized control, heterogeneity and extreme dynamism of their environment. Participants frequently join, leave and act on a best effort basis. Predictable, timely, consistent and reliable global state maintenance is infeasible. The information to be aggregated and integrated may be outdated, inconsistent, or not available at all. Failure, misbehavior, security restrictions and continuous change are the norm rather than the exception. Deployment of P2P grids is entirely user driven, obviating the need for any dedicated management of these systems. Peers expose the resources that they are willing to share (i.e. a dataset) and each resource may be replicated several times, a process that is totally decentralized and over which the original peer that advertised the resource has little or no control at all. Peers can form groups with fluid group memberships. Today, the greatest enabling factor for peer-to-peer Grid architectures is the widespread availability of high-end desktop PC or Workstation always connected to the Internet that at the state of the art offer a computational capacity of 4-6 GFlops, that is expected to become in the order of 100 GFlops within the same time frame. Such a great processing power that makes it possible to execute extremely demanding applications is largely unused (at least for the most part of the day). This opens up a very interesting window for resource sharing, also sustained by the current trend of growth of the bandwidth availability on the average and high-end Internet connections making ubiquitous Internet-based peer-to-peer Grid computing one of the most valid options available in the computing arena.

4 A Scalable Search Model in P2P Grids

The fact that today most computers in peer-to-peer grids are interconnected through the Internet give us the opportunity, in formulating our replica discovery paradigm, to exploit some of the Internet characteristics, a task that can greatly benefit from physical modeling approaches. Several empirical studies on the topology of the Internet showed that the connectivity of its nodes exhibits power law attributes and scale-free behavior in degree distribution [10]. In other words, let $P(k)$ such distribution, that is the probability that an arbitrary node be connected to exactly k other nodes:

$$P(k) = ck^{-\lambda}, \quad k \geq m \tag{1}$$

with an exponent $2 < \lambda < 3$; where c is a normalization factor and m is the minimal connectivity (usually taken to be $m = 1$). Here, we can also evidence that

$$\sum_{k=2}^{k_{max}} P(k) = 1 \tag{2}$$

where k_{max} is the maximum number of neighbors any node may have. Many naturally occurring networks (social contacts, ecological nets of predator-prey, etc.,) exhibit such degree distribution, and since several features are shared by peer-to-peer grid computing systems and these complex networks, much can be gained through integrative and comparative approaches, allowing cross-fertilization between those two important areas. Power–law networks can also be characterized by two fundamental properties [10][11]:

- a small number of links are connected by numerous nodes, while a large number of links are connected by a few nodes;
- the number of hop–counts between nodes is reduced (small–world property).

The second characteristic promotes faster propagation of information between nodes, which is a great advantage in distributed search, by optimizing the performance of the query/response traffic. However, because of the first characteristic, if several spoke nodes propagate some information at the same time or at almost the same time, the involved messages concentrate at the hub node. That is, the nodes with the very highest connectivity are subject to most of the search/query traffic. It is also likely that this tendency will increase as the number of nodes in the network increases because the number of links connected to the hub–node in turn increases. Finding a provably scalable method to search for unique content (such as the location of a replicated file) on unstructured power law networks is still an open problem. Several solutions, based on various random-walk strategies, have been proposed, but most of these reduce query traffic cost only by a constant factor. However, Power law networks are known to be an ideal platform for efficient percolation search [9], that can be a very attractive approach to ensure the needed scalability to the overall replica search/discovery system because of its relations between the probabilistic and algebraic topological properties of the Internet-based P2P organizations. According to such approach, it is always possible to overlay a scalable global-search system on this naturally scale-free graph of social contacts to enable peers to exchange their replication data efficiently. Furthermore, the query traffic cost using percolation search scales sub-linearly as a function of the system size [9]. When performing percolation search on a power–law network, we can distinguish several types of participating nodes working at different scales. Some nodes have a small number of neighbors, and thus are required to process a small number of queries passing through them. On the other end, there are nodes with large numbers of neighbors that will do a lot of work. Such search scheme implicitly makes use of high degree nodes to both cache information and respond to as much queries as possible. Thus, to achieve the best performance, one should enforce a basic form of hierarchy in the P2P Grid topological organization – that is: only high performance and huge capacity nodes have to be highly connected.

5   The Percolation Paradigm

Percolation theory [12][13] is a field of mathematics and statistical physics that provides models of phase transition phenomena that are observed in nature. Let us consider the following question, originally due to Broadbent and Hammersley, to introduce percolation theory [14]. Water is poured on one side of a large (ideally infinite) porous stone. What is the probability that the water finds a path to the opposite side? By modeling the stone as a square grid (see fig. 1 below) in which each edge can be open and hence traversed by water with probability p, and closed otherwise, independently of all other edges, one can show that for $p > 0.5$ water percolates trough the stone with probability one. One can then ask at what rate the water percolates and how it depends on. In other words, how rich in disjoint paths is the connected component of open edges? Bond percolation removes each edge in the grid with probability $1 - p$ (each edge is kept with probability p), where p is the percolation probability. The surviving edges and nodes form the percolated network.

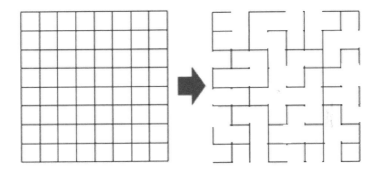

Fig. 1. Percolation on a square lattice

We can construct a mapping such that the open grid edges of a percolation model correspond to the presence of an active peering connection between the grid nodes, and the open percolating paths represent the resulting search tree on the P2P grid infrastructure that can be used to convey the requested replica location information. The percolation threshold p_c is the lowest percolation probability in which the expected size of the largest connected component goes to infinity for an infinite-size graph. If the percolation probability is lower than the percolation threshold, then the percolated network consists only of small-size connected components and lacks a giant connected component. Otherwise, if $p > p_c$ then a giant connected component emerges in the percolated network. Note that the percolation threshold is extremely small for any PL network. As a result, the size of the percolated network core is extremely small, since it is proportional to p_c. When percolation occurs above p_c, high-degree nodes are always reached during the process and become part of the giant connected component. Thus, in an unstructured P2P network search, when dataset replica information is cached in random high-degree nodes and every query originating from a random initiator node reaches and restarts from a random high-degree node, percolation can reliably find any specific dataset with an high probability (near to 1).

5.1 The Percolation Search Algorithm

Accordingly we adapted to our problem the random-walk search algorithm suggested in [9] where each node scans the contents of all its neighbors. The random walk search idea is simple: for each query, a random walker starts from the initiator and asks the nodes on the way for the requested information until it finds a match. If there are enough replicas of the needed dataset on the network, each query would be successfully answered after a few steps. In this schema, a random walker starts from a requester node to resolve a query. At each step of the walk, it scans the neighbors of the node it visits. For a power-law graph, the search quickly (with probability approaching one) converges towards high-degree nodes. Percolation search properly consists of three building blocks: *content implantation*, *query implantation*, and *bond percolation*.

Content implantation (fig. 2-a) means that every peer node in a network of n nodes announces its content through a short random walk of size $O(\log n)$ starting from itself. Only its own contents are duplicated (cached) on any node visited along the way. Clearly, highly connected nodes will develop larger caches. In fact the cache sizes obey exactly the same distribution as the degrees. The total number of contents is hence $O(n \log n)$ and the average cache size is $O(\log n)$.

A Query implantation (fig. 2-b) is executed each time a peer node issues a query. This means that the query will be "implanted" on a small number of peers through a random walk of size $O(\log n)$ starting from the requester. Content and query implantation ensure that both content (in our case a replica location information) and queries are known by at least one high-degree node, since a random walk in a power-law network gravitates towards high-degree nodes because they have a higher number of incoming links. The search is finally executed in the bond percolation step (fig. 2-c). Each peer which has an implanted query will perform a probabilistic broadcast, in which it sends the query to each of its neighbors with probability p. Probability p is set to such a value (usually a constant multiple of the percolation threshold p_c) so that a query starting from a high-degree node will be broadcast to the so-called giant component of the network (which all high-degree nodes are part of with a high probability). Clearly, if a query reaches a node which has already received the same query from another neighbor, the query is not implanted, thus avoiding loops in the query path. Since content implantation ensures that if each resource is known by at least one high-degree node, it will be found with a probability very close to 1. The information resulting from a successful search process reaches backwards the request originator node through the same path by which the query message arrived at the hit node (fig. 2-a). Every step in the algorithm is totally local and truly uniform. High degree nodes will be naturally "distilled" from on the power law network.

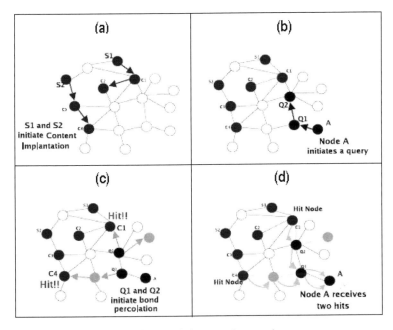

Fig. 2. Percolation search example

The search networks generated by the above algorithm form random connected graphs, where nodes are connected to few random neighbors, and have a relatively small distance between each other. The average number of hops between nodes is approximately equal to $log(n)/log(k)$, where n is the number of nodes and k is the average node degree. The existence of a small network diameter gives only a lower limit to the number of hops between two peers. The fact that the network has a power law distribution of the edges, even performing a random walk from node to node, will result in significant reduction in the number of nodes visited. This is because a random walk will tend to select high degree nodes. However, specifically choosing high degree nodes to traverse first, improves search further. Such search networks can be essentially controlled by two parameters: the exponent λ of the power–law, and the maximum degree k_{max}. Another important parameter greatly conditioning the efficiency of the whole search process is the percolation threshold p_c. In detail, in power-law networks of a finite size, the percolation threshold approaches 0 and can be calculated [15] from a degree distribution, as:

$$p_c = \frac{\langle k \rangle}{\langle k^2 \rangle - \langle k \rangle} \tag{3}$$

Here, k stands for the degree of a node, and the notation $\langle \ldots \rangle$ means the average over the degree distribution. Finally, since any content in the network can be found with probability one in time O(log n), while generating only $O(n \times \frac{2 \log k_{max}}{k_{max}})$ traffic per query, and since in random PL networks $k_{max} = c \times n$ then the overall traffic scales sub-linearly with the network size as $O(\log^2 n)$ per query [16].

5.2 Implementation Issues

While the design of the above search algorithm is based on theoretical concepts, the final formulation is straightforward and hence very easy to implement through dedicated search agents. The multi-agent technology has features well fitting for distributed communication, and is particularly robust for the interaction and negotiation tasks within P2P organizations. In a distributed agent framework, we conceptualize a dynamic community of agents, where multiple agents contribute services to the community by cooperating like individuals in a social organization. The appeal of such architectures depends on the ability of populations of agents to organize themselves and adapt dynamically to changing circumstances without top-down control from a central control logic. At first, each grid node that needs to export a dataset replica activates a specific content implantation agent that periodically starts a short random walk throughout its neighborhood and replicates on the traversed nodes the involved dataset content. Such an agent lives for the entire lifetime of each active replica. Clearly the data replication will be performed on a node along the short walk only if it is really needed (the information is not already present) and feasible (there is available space and the replica operation is locally authorized). When a job requests a specific object resource in the grid through a specific web service interface, a job-related search agent will be created. This agent will be in charge of finding candidate dataset replicas through the proposed percolation-based interactions, lives until the associated search task executes and will be dissolved when it is finished and the replica results are sent to the requesting node and cached on the intermediate nodes along the search tree. Clearly, an aging timeout is associated to each cached replica so that when such a timeout expires and the information has not been refreshed by another content implantation or during the backward query/response process, the entry is no longer valid and hence deleted. It should be noted that a search agent might be involved in several query implantation activities during the same percolation search process. Since cooperation, negotiation, and competition are natural activities common in multi-agent systems the above content and query implantation functionalities and the following percolation search process are naturally implemented by using the agent oriented approach. The percolation search network needs to be overlaid on top of the peer-to-peer interactions between the grid nodes built during both the content implantation and query processing activities and the involved agents cooperate by implementing the above search steps by interacting through an existing P2P grid communication paradigm. Communication between neighbor peers can be enabled by existing P2P interaction facilities such as JXTA [17] (from juxtaposition) or P2PS [18] (Peer-to-Peer Simplified) protocols. JXTA provides features such as dynamic discovery while allowing peers to communicate across NAT, DHCP, and firewall boundaries. It is independent of transport protocols and can be implemented on top of TCP/IP, HTTP, TLS, and many other protocols. P2PS is a lightweight infrastructure for developing P2P style applications whose architecture is inspired to and provides a subset of functionality of JXTA. In both the solutions a peer is any node that supports the specific interaction protocols and could be any digital device. Peers publish the existence of a dataset resource through an advertisement, which is simply an XML document describing the resource. Interactions between agent peers are self-attenuating, with interactions dying out after a certain number of hops. These attenuations in tandem with traces of the peers, which the interactions have passed through, eliminate the continuous echoing problem that results from loops in peer connectivity. In such environment, the specific agents described before will be implemented at the P2P Grid middleware level on each local grid node involved in the above percolation-based replica discovery and management framework. These agents provide a high-level representation of the corresponding search or replica location notification capability. Hence, they also characterize the available dataset resources as information service providers in a wider grid environment. Agents can be structured within the proposed architecture according to a simple layered model (see fig. 3).

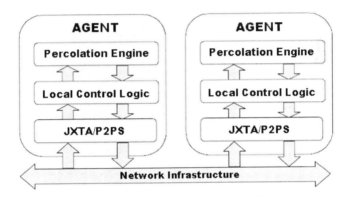

Fig. 3. The generic agent layered structure

Here we can distinguish a bottommost communication layer, implemented through the above JXTA or P2PS facilities, realizing all the Agent-to-Agent interactions and peer communication mechanisms. An intermediate local control layer is needed for all the authorization and management tasks to be autonomously performed at the individual node level (local resources management, authorization and access-control policies enforcing, data replication etc.). Finally, a "percolation engine" at the uppermost layer realizes all the main specialized agent functionalities, starting from implementing the random walks for content implantation to replica information caching and performing percolation search through "probabilistic broadcast" query implantation activities and backward result propagation.

6 Functional Evaluation

In order to evaluate our model through simulation, we generated a random network with a power law link distribution by using the Pajek [19] environment. The generation process is based on generalized Barabasi-Albert construction model [20], which presumes that every vertex has at least some baseline probability of gaining an edge, to generate edges by mixture of preferential attachment and uniform attachment. For generating condition, we set the total node number to 30000, $\lambda=2$ and a maximum degree of 6. We worked with a TTL value varying from 15 to 25. Such parameter can be thought as an upper bound of hops on the query implantation. In order to evaluate the results, we analyzed under varying percolation probabilities the behavior of the following three metrics expressed as percentage values: the success rate in finding an object, the number of edges and the number of nodes traversed throughout the search process. We first evaluated our replica search algorithm with a single copy of a content randomly located on the network (Fig. 4).

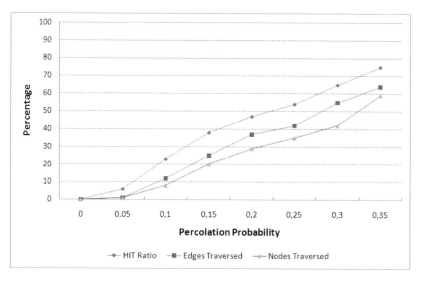

Fig. 4. Simulation results with 1 replica, TTL=15

Here no content implantation step is performed by the owner node and no information is cached throughout the network during the search process. We can observe that the percolation search mechanism is however effective but it really converges only when percolation probability approaches to 0.4 and an unacceptably high number of nodes and edges are traversed to reach the needed content. In fact the hit ratio and the traversed edges/nodes trends grow together almost linearly with the percolation probability. Next we also considered another relevant issue: what would be the improvement in performance if multiple high degree nodes in the network had the same content so that the above percolation paradigm may be really effective. Accordingly as a part of the percolation search algorithm, we execute both the initial content implantation and the following caching steps that make sure that any subsequent query step would find any content with probability approaching one. Figure 5 below shows the case where 10 replicas of any content are randomly spread in the network. We can note that, in presence of a sufficient number of replicated contents, also a slight increment in percolation probability improves the hit rate exponentially until it rapidly reaches 100%.

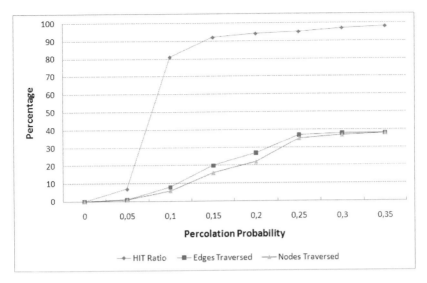

Fig. 5. Simulation results with 10 replicas, TTL=15

7   Conclusion

This work focuses on searching for replicated objects (files, resources, etc.) in fully decentralized P2P grids, i.e., where a (large) set of peers, can exchange information in absence of any central service. Accordingly we propose a scalable search model for such totally unstructured grids based on a known algorithm that uses random-walks and bond percolation on random graphs with heavy-tailed degree distributions to provide access to any content on any node with probability one. We analyzed the validity of our model and examined its dynamics through simulations. We can conclude that our proposal can be effective in both reducing the total amount of queries/checks and ensuring an high success rate, which means we can provide a robust and effective search platform for emerging P2P grid infrastructures.

References

1. Botros, S., Waterhouse, S.: Search in JXTA and other distributed networks. In: P2P Computing conference (2001)
2. Ratnasamy, S., Francis, P., Handley, M., Karp, R., Shenker, S.: A scalable content addressable Network. In: ACM SIGCOM (2001)
3. Dabek, F., Brunskill, E., Kaashoek, M.F., Karger, D., Morris, R., Stoica, I., Balakrishnan, H.: Building peer-to-peer systems with Chord, a Distributed Lookup Service (2001), http://pdos.lcs.mit.edu/chord
4. Zhao, B.Y., Kubiatowicz, I., Joseph, A.: Tapestry: An infrastructure for fault-tolerant wide area location and routing", Computer Science Department, UCB Report UCB/CSD-O 1-1141 (2001)
5. Lv, Q., Cohen, E., Li, K., Shenker, S.: Search and Replication in unstructured peer-to-peer network. In: International Conference on Supercomputing (2002)

6. Gkantsidis, C., Mihail, M., Saberi, A.: Hybrid Search Schemes for Unstructured Peer-to-Peer Networks. In: IEEE Infocom 2005. IEEE CS Press, Los Alamitos (2005)
7. Adamic, L.A., Lukose, R.M., Puniyani, A.R., Huberman, B.A.: Search in Power-Law Networks. Physical Review E 64 (2001)
8. Gkantsidis, C., Mihail, M., Saberi, A.: Random Walks in Peer-to-Peer Networks. In: IEEE INFOCOM 2004, Hong Kong, China (2004)
9. Sarshar, N., Roychowdury, V., Boykin, P.O.: Percolation search algorithm, making unstructured p2p networks scalable. In: Fourth IEEE P2P 2004, Zurich, Switzerland. IEEE Computer Society Press, Los Alamitos (2004)
10. Faloutsos, M., Faloutsos, P., Faloutsos, C.: On power–law relationships of the Internet topology. In: Proceedings of ACM SIGCOMM 1999, October 1999, pp. 251–262 (1999)
11. Barabasi, A., Albert, R.: Emergence of scaling in random networks. Science 286, 509–512 (1999)
12. Grimmett, G.: Percolation, 2nd edn. Springer, New York (1999)
13. Meester, R., Roy, R.: Continuum Percolation. Cambridge Univ. Press, Cambridge (1996)
14. Broadbent, S.R., Hammersley, J.M.: Percolation processes in Crystals and mazes. Proc. Cambridge Philosoph. Soc. 53, 629–641 (1957)
15. Newman, M.E.J.: The structure and function of complex networks. SIAM Review 45(2), 167–256 (2003)
16. Sarshar, N., Boykin, P.O., Roychowdury, V.: Scalable percolation search on complex networks. Theoretical Computer Science 355, 48–64 (2006)
17. Sun Microsystems. The JXTA project and peer-to-peer technology (November 2004), http://www.jxta.org
18. Wang: P2PS (Peer-to-Peer Simplified. In: 13th Conference - Frontiers of Grid Applications and Technologies, Louisiana State University, pp. 54–59 (2005)
19. Pajek project, http://vlado.fmf.uni-lj.si/pub/networks/pajek
20. Albert, R., Barabasi, A.: Topology of Evolving Networks: Local Events and Universality. Phys. Rev. Lett. 85, 5234–5237 (2000)

GridFTP GUI: An Easy and Efficient Way to Transfer Data in Grid

Wantao Liu[1,2], Rajkumar Kettimuthu[3,4], Brian Tieman[5], Ravi Madduri[3,4], Bo Li[1], and Ian Foster[2,3,4]

[1] School of Computer Science and Engineering, Beihang University, Beijing, China
[2] Department of Computer Science, The University of Chicago, Chicago, IL USA
[3] Mathematics and Computer Science Division, Argonne National Laboratory, Argonne, IL USA
[4] Computation Institute, The University of Chicago, Chicago, IL USA
[5] Advanced Photon Source, Argonne National Laboratory, Argonne, IL USA
liuwt@uchicago.edu, kettimut@mcs.anl.gov, tieman@aps.anl.gov,
madduri@mcs.anl.gov, libo@act.buaa.edu.cn, foster@mcs.anl.gov

Abstract. GridFTP is the de facto standard for providing secure, robust, high-speed bulk data transport. It is based on the Internet FTP protocol, and it defines extensions for high performance operation and security. However, GridFTP lacks an easy-to-use graphical user interface client that is fault tolerant and hides all the complexities from the end users. It is not straightforward to conduct data transfer, monitor transfer status, and recover from transfer errors. Many e-science applications must transfer large datasets that are, in many cases, are partitioned into lots of small files. However, existing GridFTP client tools cannot do such a transfer efficiently and reliably. To address these issues, we developed GridFTP GUI, a Java web start-based GridFTP client tool. It does not require explicit installation and can automatically update to the latest version. It provides an easy and efficient way for users to get credentials, transfer data through drag and drop, optimize transfer parameters, view transfer progress, move a lot of small files in an efficient way, recover from transfer errors, manage files and directories remotely, and establish cross-domain trust relationships. Our experiments show that GridFTP GUI is able to transfer files and directories with very good performance.

Keywords: GridFTP, data transfer.

1 Introduction

The GridFTP [1] protocol is widely used in Grid environments. It extends the standard FTP [2] protocol for high-performance operation and security. The Globus implementation of GridFTP [3] provides a modular and extensible data transfer system architecture suitable for wide-area and high-performance environments. GridFTP achieves good performance by using non-TCP protocols such as UDT [10] and parallel streams to minimize bottlenecks inherent in TCP [11]. GridFTP can also do coordinated data transfer by using multiple computer nodes at the source and destination. Globus GridFTP supports various security options, including Grid Security

T. Doulamis et al.: (Eds.): GridNets 2009, LNICST 25, pp. 57–66, 2010.

Infrastructure (GSI), username/password authentication provided by regular FTP servers, and SSH-based security.

Many scientific experiments produce hundreds of thousands of files to transfer every day. The individual file size is modest, typically on the order of kilobytes or megabytes, but the size of the entire dataset for each experiment is tremendous, ranging from hundreds of gigabytes to hundreds of terabytes. For example, tomography experiments on the Advanced Photon Source at Argonne National Laboratory produce hundreds of gigabytes of data every day. The datasets are typically organized into a hierarchical directory. The number of files under each subdirectory is moderate; however, the total number of files under a top-level directory that needs to be moved is huge. In a typical day, dozens of samples may be acquired; each sample generates about 2,000 raw data files. After processing, each sample produces additional 2,000 reconstructed files; each file is 8 to 16 MB in size.

Many scientists use GridFTP to transfer their experimental data from sites where experiments are conducted to computational sites where the acquired data is analyzed. After the data has been processed, the output data must be archived at other sites. Globus-url-copy is a commonly used GridFTP client. Since it is a command-line tool, typically scripts are used to perform the cited tasks. Because discipline scientists often have only limited computer knowledge and experience, dealing with scripts and command-line interfaces is difficult and tedious. Contending with cross-platform issues, tuning performance parameters, recovering from transfer errors, and managing files and directories in remote GridFTP servers make the process even more difficult. The scientific research user communities need a tool for GridFTP data transfer and management that provides the following features:

1. Ease of use: It should not take much time to learn how to use this tool. A graphical user interface therefore is preferable to a command-line interface.

2. Monitoring: Users should be able to monitor the status of the transfers.

3. Remote file management: Users should be able to manage the remote files and directories by performing operations such as create/delete remote files and directories.

4. Performance tuning: The tool should support automated and manual tuning of parameters to improve performance.

5. Error recovery: The tool should be able to recover from any failures and restart transfers automatically.

6. Efficiency: Data movement activity is an integral part of the scientific experiments, a significant part in many cases. If the tool is not efficient enough, it will impact the whole experiment significantly.

GridFTP GUI, a cross-platform client tool for GridFTP, has these six features. It has a simple and familiar interface; hence, users do not take long to learn how to use it. GridFTP GUI is based on Java web start technology [4]. Users can get it by clicking a link in a web page; the program will be downloaded and started automatically. There is no explicit installation process.

The paper is organized as follows. In Section 2, we review related work. Section 3 presents the design and implementation of GridFTP GUI. In Section 4, we discuss experimental results. Section 5 presents conclusions and future work.

2   Related Work

RFT (Reliable Transfer Service) [8] is a component of the Globus Toolkit. Implemented as a set of Grid services, RFT performs third-party transfers using GridFTP with basic reliable mechanisms. Data transfer state is dumped into database; if a transfer fails, it can be restarted automatically from the broken point by using the persistent data. RFT offers a command-line client for end users to conduct reliable third-party transfers. GridFTP GUI is a lightweight client that supports both client-server and third-party GridFTP transfers. Also, the GridFTP GUI has been integrated with RFT to provide better fault-tolerant capability for third-party transfers.

GridCopy [12] is a command-line client for GridFTP. It accepts SCP-style source and destination specifications. GridCopy translates the SCP-style pathnames into appropriate GridFTP URLs. Moreover, it is able to calculate an optimal value of TCP buffer size and parallel TCP streams for the GridFTP transfer to maximize throughput. But it does not provide an easy way to manage remote files. Also, GridFTP GUI provides better fault-tolerant capability than does GridCopy.

Topaz [5] is an extension of the Firefox browser to enable GridFTP capability. This work is based on Mozilla framework. However, because of the limitations of the browser, Topaz implements only file download and upload. Other features of GridFTP are not supported; remote file management is not supported as well.

UberFTP [6] is an interactive shell GridFTP client. It supports GSI authentication, parallel data channels and third party transfer. UberFTP is not able to conduct reliable file transfer, however, whereas GridFTP GUI incorporates with RFT service to offer reliability in file transfers.

GridFTP Client [7] is an eclipse-based Java application. It is distributed as a standalone application or an eclipse plug-in. It is able to transfer a directory that includes a lot of nested subdirectories, create and delete remote files and directories, monitor transfer status. However, GridFTP Client supports only third-party transfers; thus, users cannot download or upload files between GridFTP server and GridFTP Client.

The CoG jglobus [13] library includes a pure Java GridFTP client API. It can be used to build applications that communicate with GridFTP servers. It supports client-server transfers, third-party transfers, parallel streams and TCP buffer size setting, striping, GSI authentication, and other features. GridFTP GUI uses CoG jglobus to communicate with GridFTP servers.

3   GridFTP GUI Design and Implementation

The heterogeneity of Grid environments is reflected not only in the server side but also in the client side. Users requesting Grid resources run on a great diversity of platforms. Hence, cross-platform issues must be taken into account when designing and implementing Grid client software. For the GUI to operate on a variety of platforms, we have developed the GUI in the Java programming language.

Since our aim is to enable the average user easily to perform GridFTP transfers, we adopted the Java web start technology. With Java web start, the user can access the application with a single click. The application is then downloaded to user's client machine and installed to a system-dependent location for the first time launch. For subsequent uses, the user can just invoke the application on his machine. Java web start automatically checks whether the application has a new version in the software repository; if so, it downloads the new version without user intervention. Users can always get the most recent version of the application without any manual installation.

Obtaining certificates and setting up GSI are difficult tasks for an average user. The GridFTP GUI has been integrated with MyProxy [9] to reduce the burden of managing certificates. MyProxy is an X509 PKI credential management service that enables users to upload their credentials to an online credential repository and obtain them when needed. MyProxy also can act as a certificate authority (CA). Virtual organizations can use its CA capability to issue certificates to their users. It can be configured in such a way that the users can obtain the certificates by typing in a username and password. With GridFTP GUI, users do not need to explicitly obtain or handle the certificate from the MyProxy server. Through the GUI, users can authenticate with the MyProxy server using a username and password and let the GUI handle the retrieval and setting up of the certificates.

3.1   Design of GridFTP GUI

GridFTP GUI is modular. Its architecture is presented in Figure 1. The topmost layer is an assembly of graphical user interface elements; specifically, they are Java Swing controls, which are responsible for interaction with users. This layer is divided into several parts in terms of functionality:

- *Cred Manager* is used for credential management. It interacts with MyProxy and local GSI credential files. Users can generate and destroy credentials and view credential information.
- *Login Manager* accepts user specified GridFTP server name and port, constructs commands that are used for GridFTP login and pass them to command executor.
- *File Browser* controls how local and remote files are displayed; tree view is implemented currently. It supports navigation among different file hierarchies. Users can create directories and delete or move files or directories through file browser. Moreover, users can drag and drop files or directories among file browsers to trigger GridFTP data transfer.
- *Status Manager* provides a view for users to see the status of completed transfers and the progress of on-going transfers.
- *Config Manager* is responsible for configuration of GridFTP parameters, such as the TCP buffer size or parallel streams, via a graphical interface.
- *Log Manager* allows the user *to* set the log file location and views log file.

Figure 2 shows a snapshot of GridFTP GUI. The command executor component, receives user commands passed from the upper-layer GUI elements and executes them. Commands are divided into two categories: control commands and transfer commands. Control commands control the behavior of GridFTP GUI (e.g., open a file browser, generate a new proxy) and do not interact with the GridFTP server. The command executor executes these commands immediately for timely response. Transfer commands instruct the GridFTP server or RFT service to finish some tasks; they

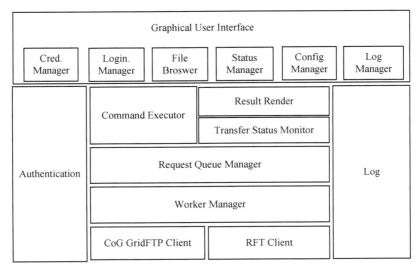

Fig. 1. Components of GridFTP GUI

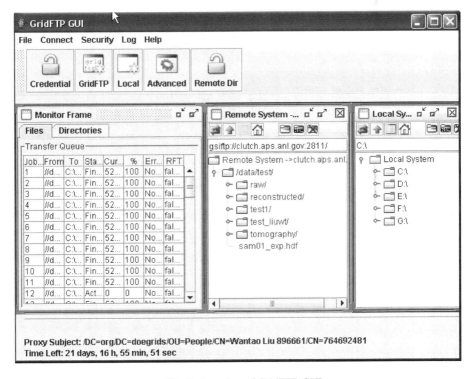

Fig. 2. Snapshot of GridFTP GUI

are put into a queue managed by the request queue manager. Since there are two types of commands, the command executor is designed as an abstract interface, which has different concrete implementations to handle corresponding types of commands. This design facilitates the extensibility of the program.

The request queue manager uses a specific policy for queuing transfer requests. Currently, only the first come first serve (FCFS) policy is implemented. All requests in the request queue are processed by worker threads in a thread pool. These threads are managed by the worker manager, which assigns requests for different workers and monitors the execution of these threads. According to different commands, worker threads invoke the CoG jglobus client or RFT client for data transfer.

The transfer status monitor is used for checking transfer status and progress. The status information is then passed to the result renderer, which can display this information in different ways.

3.2   Handling Large Numbers of Files

Moving a lot of files from one location to another is a requirement in e-science. To reach high-throughput levels, conventional GridFTP clients require not only that the amount of data to transfer be large enough to allow TCP to reach full throttle but also that the data be in large files, ideally in one single file. If the dataset is large but partitioned into many small files (on gigabit networks we consider any file smaller than 100 MB as a small file), the performance suffers drastically. To address this issue, we use a pool of transfer worker threads to handle the request queue. Multiple files are moved concurrently to maximize the utilization of network bandwidth and thus improve the transfer performance.

Displaying transfer status clearly and methodically in the GUI when moving a lot of files is a challenging task as well. The GUI needs to provide users well-organized information so that the users can easily view the status of the transfer. Based on these considerations, we use two Java Swing JPanels to show transfer information. One JPanel lists all directories and their transfer status; the other JPanel lists all files under the active directory. This solution offers users an easy way to know the overall transfer status and progress of a specific file.

When the program starts moving a directory that contains subdirectories and a lot of files, the directory is traversed recursively, and only nested subdirectory nodes are returned and put into a queue. All these nested subdirectory nodes are added to the directory transfer panel. After the traversal, queued subdirectory nodes are tackled in FCFS order. For a subdirectory node, all the regular files under the subdirectory are retrieved and added to the file transfer request panel. After retrieval of a subdirectory, a corresponding transfer request is constructed for each regular file and put into the request queue. When a transfer request status changes, the file transfer request panel updates the corresponding entry. Since the request queue size is limited, when the queue is full, the thread that is putting requests into the queue is suspended until there is space again.

We retrieve all regular files of a subdirectory only after all the files in the previous subdirectory are transferred. Thus, significant delay could occur between the retrieval of the file list in one subdirectory and the retrieval of the file list in the next subdirectory. Hence, the GridFTP control connection could time out. To keep the control connection alive, we implemented a thread that periodically sends a NOOP command to the GridFTP server.

3.3   Error Recovery

Errors can occur during data transfer for various reasons, such as disk failure, network outage, and end system problems. While transferring a lot of individual files or a directory with lots of files, it would be tedious to have to manually identify and re-transfer the files that had not been transferred successfully. Therefore, automatic recovery from errors is an important feature.

GridFTP GUI supports automatic error recovery capabilities. The GUI will retry any failed transfers. The number of retries and the interval between subsequent retries can be configured. Also, the GUI stores the necessary status information on the local file system so that the transfer can be resumed seamlessly after a local failure, such as an unexpected GUI crash or client machine failure. The GUI has also been integrated with RFT to provide more robust fault-tolerant capabilities. RFT stores the transfer state in a persistent store.

3.4   Establishment of Cross-Domain Trust Relationships

In Grid environments, data commonly is transferred among participants located in different organizations, countries, or even continents, each having individual policies and trust certificates issued by distinct accredited authorities. Hence, establishing trust relationships is a big challenge for users conducting cross-domain communication.

The International Grid Trust Federation (IGTF) [14] is an organization that federates policy management authorities all over the world, with the goal of enhancing establishment of cross-domain trust relationships between Grid participants. The distribution provided by IGTF contains root certificates, certificate revocation list locations, contact information, and signing of policies. Users can download this distribution and install it to conduct cross-domain communication.

GridFTP GUI interacts with IGTF. When GridFTP GUI starts up, it contacts IGTF's website and checks the available distribution to see whether there is any update. The latest distribution will be downloaded and installed into the directory where the user puts the certificates. This feature simplifies the user's effort in establishing cross-domain trust relationships with other Grid entities.

4   Performance Evaluation

In this section, we present some performance evaluation results of GridFTP GUI compared with scp and globus-url-copy. Scp [15] is a widely used command line tool for remote data transfer with security. It is able to copy files between hosts on a network and provides the same security as ssh. Globus-url-copy [16] is a command line GridFTP client shipped with Globus Toolkit. Globus-url-copy supports multiple parallel data streams for a single transfer; this feature can dramatically improve performance when transferring a big file. This optimization parameter is used in our experiment. Because of the broad acceptance of the two tools, they are selected to compare with GridFTP GUI.

We conducted all of our experiments using TeraGrid NCSA nodes and the University of Chicago nodes. Each experiment was run three times, and the average value is presented here. The GridFTP servers involved in the experiments were configured to use TCP as the underlying data transport protocol; scp uses TCP as well. As stated above, globus-url-copy is able to establish multiple data streams to transfer a single file; in the following charts, "globus-url-copy(p=4)" refers to four data streams for a single file transfer. Besides parallel streams, GridFTP GUI can transfer multiple different files simultaneously through its transfer worker thread pool; the thread pool size was set to four in all experiments. "GridFTP GUI(p=4)" denotes each worker thread has four data streams, and "GridFTP GUI" denotes each worker thread has only one data stream.

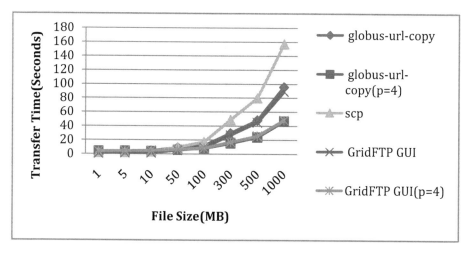

Fig. 3. Data transfer time of a single file (from NCSA to UChicago)

In the first experiment, we examined the time consumed to transfer a single file. In this experiment, after a file transfer was finished, we requested another file transfer. Eight file sizes were used: 1 MB, 5 MB, 10 MB, 50 MB, 100 MB, 300 MB, 500 MB, and 1000 MB. Data was moved from NCSA to the University of Chicago. Figure 3 shows the results of this experiment. We can see that the five curves are very close when the data size is less than 10 MB. After that, both globus-url-copy and GridFTP GUI with four data streams outperforms other programs remarkably. It should be noted that GridFTP GUI's performance is as good as globus-url-copy. Though the default number of worker threads is set to four, only one thread is used here as this experiment involved only single file transfers.

Figure 4 and 5 demonstrate performance for directory. In the two experiments, only globus-url-copy with four data streams and GridFTP GUI with one data stream for each worker thread are examined (in Figure 4, scp is compared as well). Figure 4 shows the data transfer time of a directory with tens of thousands of small files. It is a simulation of a typical scenario in e-science. In this evaluation, we created directories of 10,000, 20,000, 30,000, 40,000 and 50,000 files. Each file was 1 MB. Therefore, the total data size moved ranged from 10 GB to 50 GB. Data flowed from the

University of Chicago to NCSA. From the plot, we can see that GridFTP GUI remarkably outperforms scp and globus-url-copy with four streams. The multiple concurrent transfer threads in GUI help it achieve superior performance while transferring directories with lots of small files. Globus-url-copy can use multiple concurrent transfers to achieve performance similar to that of GUI. Still, GUI will be much more easier to use for the scientific community than globus-url-copy.

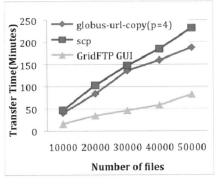 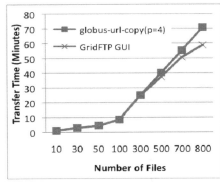

Fig. 4. Transfer of directory containing lots of 1 MB files (from UChicago to NCSA)

Fig. 5. Transfer of directory containing 100 MB files (from UChicago to NCSA)

To investigate the performance of GridFTP GUI when moving a directory with large files, we carried out another experiment. A directory with different number of files was moved from the University of Chicago to NCSA; each file was 100 MB. The number of files in a directory ranged from 10 to 800. As depicted in Fig. 5, GridFTP GUI shows moderate improvement compared with globus-url-copy with four parallel streams.

5   Conclusions and Future Work

In this paper, we presented GridFTP GUI, a comprehensive GridFTP client that enables using users to generate a proxy certificate or obtain it from MyProxy, conduct client/server or third-party data transfers by drag and drop, view transfer progress, set GridFTP server parameters, manage files and directories in remote GridFTP servers, and recover from transfer errors automatically. GridFTP GUI is a Java web start application; hence, no explicit installation process is required, and the program can automatically update to the latest version.

We plan to implement more sophisticated ways of managing transfer requests. In the current implementation, all transfer requests are put into the queue in FCFS order. Since priority of data transfer request is important in some cases, however, we are going to add more sophisticated queuing policies to support priority. Another enhancement we intend to make is to automatically optimize transfer parameters. Configuring transfer parameter is not easy for users, and the optimal value of those parameters is affected by multiple factors. Hence, it will be helpful if GridFTP GUI can automatically optimize transfer parameters. In [12], a practical approach for GridFTP transfer parameter estimation is proposed. We plan to use that approach as a starting point to provide this capability.

Acknowledgments

This work was supported in part by the Office of Advanced Scientific Computing Research, Office of Science, U.S. Department of Energy, under Contract DE-AC02-06CH11357.

References

1. Allcock, W.: GridFTP: Protocol Extension to FTP for the Grid. In: Global Grid Forum GFDR- P.020 (2003)
2. Postel, J., Reynolds, J.: File Transfer Protocol. IETF, RFC 959 (1985)
3. Allcock, W., Bresnahan, J., Kettimuthu, R., Link, M., Dumitrescu, C., Raicu, I., Foster, I.: The Globus Striped GridFTP Framework and Server. In: SC 2005. ACM Press, New York (2005)
4. Java Web Start, http://java.sun.com/javase/technologies/desktop/javawebstart/index.jsp
5. Zamudio, R., Catarino, D., Taufer, M., Bhatia, K., Stearn, B.: Topaz:Extending Firefox to Accommodate the GridFTP Protocol. In: Proceedings of the Fourth High-Performance Grid Computing Workshop HPGC 2007, in conjunction with IPDPS 2007, Long Beach, California (March 2007)
6. Uberftp, http://dims.ncsa.uiuc.edu/set/uberftp/
7. GridFTP Client, http://bi.offis.de/gridftp/downloads.html
8. RFT, http://globus.org/toolkit/docs/latest-able/data/rft/#rft
9. MyProxy, http://grid.ncsa.uiuc.edu/myproxy/
10. Gu, Y., Grossman, R.L.: UDT: UDP-based Data Transfer for High-Speed Wide Area Networks. Comput. Networks 51(7), 1777–1799 (2007)
11. Postel, J.: Transmission Control Protocol. IETF, RFT 793 (September 1981)
12. Kettimuthu, R., Allcock, W., Liming, L., Navarro, J., Foster, I.: GridCopy: Moving Data Fast on the Grid. In: Fourth High Performance Grid Computing Workshop HPGC 2007, in conjunction with IPDPS 2007, Long Beach, California (March 2007)
13. CoG jglobus, http://dev.globus.org/wiki/CoG_jglobus
14. IGTF, http://www.igtf.net/
15. Scp, http://en.wikipedia.org/wiki/Secure_copy
16. GridFTP, http://www.globus.org/toolkit/docs/4.0/data/gridftp/rn01re01.html

Part III

General Session 3

An Alarms Service for Monitoring Multi-domain Grid Networks

Charaka Palansuriya, Jeremy Nowell, Florian Scharinger, Kostas Kavoussanakis, and Arthur S. Trew

EPCC, The University of Edinburgh,
Mayfield Road, Edinburgh, EH9 3JZ, UK
{charaka,jeremy,florian,kavousan,arthur}@epcc.ed.ac.uk

Abstract. Effective monitoring of multi-domain Grid networks is essential to support large operational Grid infrastructures. Timely detection of network problems is an essential part of this monitoring. In order to detect the problems, access to network monitoring data that exists in multiple organisations is necessary. This paper presents an Alarms Service that supports monitoring of such multi-domain Grid networks. The service allows timely detection of networking problems based on pre-defined, user-configurable conditions. The requirements gathered from real users for monitoring the networks are discussed. The paper shows how multi-organisation data access is resolved with the use of a standards-based access mechanism. The architecture of the Alarms Service is discussed, providing the reasons behind the design decisions where appropriate. A description of the current implementation of the Alarms Service and its deployment is provided.

Keywords: Alarms, multi-domain networks, Grid, federated networks, network monitoring, Network Monitoring Working Group (NM-WG).

1 Introduction

Grid infrastructures rely on networks as a fundamental component. Large Grid infrastructures are typically composed of many different federated network domains, covering local campus networks, National Research and Education Networks (NRENs), and continental scale research networks such as GÉANT2. Effective monitoring of these federated networks is fundamental in maintaining efficient operational Grids. However, different network domains are typically heterogeneous in both their administration and operation, and may be monitored using a variety of different software tools. Access to the network monitoring data gathered within each domain by these different tools is essential to provide a Grid-wide view of network health.

Our previous work [1] focused on providing access to heterogeneous federated network monitoring data, making use of standards developed by the OGF Network Measurements Working Group (NM-WG) [2]. During the course of this work it became clear that there was a strong requirement for alarms to be raised based on the network status. Grid and network operators need access to network monitoring data to diagnose problems in the network, but just as importantly they need alarms to notify

T. Doulamis et al.: (Eds.): GridNets 2009, LNICST 25, pp. 69–78, 2010.

them of such problems as soon as they occur. Therefore, we have developed a software framework that accesses network monitoring data, analyses the data collected, and raises alarms based on pre-defined, user-configurable conditions. We call this software framework the "Alarms Service". The service allows the timely detection and trouble-shooting of networking problems, reducing the chances of users of the networks encountering the problems (or symptoms of the problems) before the operators.

The requirements for the Alarms Service described in this paper have been largely gathered from members of the Large Hadron Collider Optical Private Network (LHCOPN) [3]. The architecture developed uses sources of data such as those provided by perfSONAR [4], and uses NM-WG standards to access the data. An implementation of the Alarms Service has been developed based on this architecture to monitor the LHCOPN and to obtain feedback from network operators and other potential users.

This paper describes various technical aspect of the Alarms Service. The remainder of the paper is organised as follows. Section 2 describes the motivation behind the work; section 3 highlights the requirements gathered from the users and network operators; section 4 provides a detailed description of the architecture; section 5 describes the current implementation; section 6 mentions the present deployment; and finally section 7 provides conclusions and future work.

2 Motivation

The motivation for the Alarms Service work came from speaking to various network operators during our previous work. The discussions revealed that it is both unrealistic and too demanding for operators of Grid and Network Operating Centres (GOCs and NOCs respectively) to continuously monitor their networks using historical data. They require an alarm system that is capable of alerting them to networking problems as they arise. These problems can then be investigated in detail using the other tools available to them.

Since the different parts of a federated network belong to different organisations, the first issue that operators face is how to access network monitoring data from other organisations, for example SNMP access to remote routers is not allowed. Due to such data access issues, it is difficult to use off the shelf alarm systems. The data access mechanism used by the Alarms Service is therefore a fundamental part of its architecture, providing a solution to the problem of cross-domain data sharing.

Network operators do not want to be restricted in their choice of network monitoring framework. This presents another issue to be solved in order to gain access to the monitoring data that is necessary to analyse for alarms conditions. That is, how to access monitoring data collected by heterogeneous monitoring frameworks. Clearly, a standard interface such as the one developed by the NM-WG group is necessary.

Even with a standard interface, access to data sources at different locations and belonging to various organisations is necessary. This requires knowledge about the location of relevant data sources, access restrictions and so on.

A combination of different data sources is necessary to monitor certain alarm conditions. For example, router output packet drops may be stored in one data source whilst utilisation is stored in another. A combined analysis of monitoring data for the two metrics is necessary, for example, to work out whether there is some network fault, rather than high utilisation, causing output drops. The necessary integration of these data sources is not trivial in a Grid or a federated network.

The above factors led to a ground-up development of an alarms framework. Prior to commencing the development work more specific user requirements were gathered.

3 Requirements

A list of prioritized alarm conditions were gathered from the operators of the LHCOPN. Indeed, the LHCOPN will be the first user of the Alarms Service. The most important conditions were determined to be as follows:

1. Routing Alarm: If the path, as determined by traceroute [5], changes and there are no network links down between the source and destination, then raise an alarm.
2. Routing Out of Network Alarm: If the path changes and one of the hops is outside the preferred (federated) network, then raise an alarm.
3. Interface Errors Alarm: If a router interface has input errors at a rate above a threshold then raise an alarm.
4. Interface Congestion Alarm: If a router interface drops packets at a rate above a threshold, whilst the link utilisation is below another threshold, then raise an alarm.

LHCOPN stated that the Routing Alarm is the most important since no suitable tool is available to monitor this condition. This alarm would indicate a possible re-route over another Tier1[1] site, thereby overburdening that site and affecting the network performance.

The Routing Out of Network Alarm was also indicated as essential, since this would signal that the network traffic is being routed outside the fast (10 Gbps) Optical Private Network (OPN) and there will be a significant performance degradation. There are also issues such as security, confidentiality and violation of Service Level Agreements (SLAs) to consider when such a routing problem occurs.

The Interface Errors Alarm was indicated as essential since it flags circuit errors that need to be investigated by the Network Operation Centres (NOCs). The LHCOPN needs to sustain very fast (several Gbps) data flows to support the transfer of the huge amount of data produced by the LHC at the Tier0 site at CERN to the Tier1 sites. If there are any interface errors then this will lead to packet drops, making it difficult to achieve the required performance.

The Interface Congestion Alarm was indicated as useful as this would indicate other network faults, apart from high network utilisation, causing output drops and thereby impacting data flow speed.

Further requirements for an Alarms Service were generated with the help of the LHCOPN as well as DANTE [6] and WiN-Labor [7]. In addition to the alarm conditions themselves, these include requirements that the status of the alarms MUST [8] be accessible via a web-based dashboard, and that an alarm SHOULD display what

---

[1] Note that data from CERN, i.e., Tier0, gets distributed to first level processing and storage centres called Tier1.

action is to be pursued to solve the problem. Users SHOULD be notified of alarms when they arise, for example via email. Another important requirement is that the alarm conditions as well as their threshold values MUST be configurable. Due to the distributed nature of the network monitoring data on which the alarms are raised, the alarm service MUST be able to access multiple data sources. The history of alarms SHOULD be available.

4   Architecture

4.1   Overview

The above motivating factors and requirements led to the development of the architecture shown in Fig. 1.

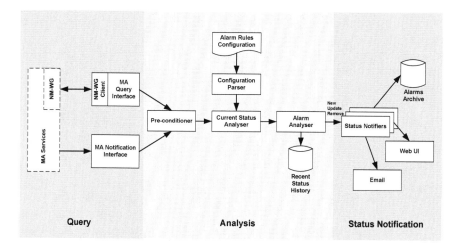

Fig. 1. The Alarms Service Architecture

The Alarms Service expects to utilise various external sources of network measurement data, known as Measurement Archives (MAs), shown in dotted lines in Fig. 1. The data may be obtained from an MA on request via the MA Query Interface; or alternatively by allowing a data source to send status updates via the MA Notification interface. This latter case is especially interesting if the data source already does some processing of the underlying measurement data, and is able to determine if there is a problem itself. The data received by the MA Query Interface and the MA Notification Interface is fed into the Pre-Conditioner component for cleaning. The Pre-Conditioner performs various tasks such as removal of any *outliers* (i.e., a single measurement can be significantly off the norm and does not qualify for an alarm to be raised) [9] and then presents data to the Current Status Analyser. The Current Status Analyser uses the cleaned up measurement data along with the configuration details (e.g., alarm conditions and how often to analyse) to check whether an alarm condition has been reached. When an alarm condition is reached, the Current Status Analyser informs the Alarm Analyser. The Alarm Analyser checks the Recent Status History store to detect whether it is a new alarm, if it was already detected or if an existing alarm is not valid anymore. The Alarm Analyser can also be used to detect conditions such as *flapping* (i.e., when an alarm rapidly changes state between on and off). The Alarm Analyser informs registered notifiers about status changes (new, update or remove alarm). Multiple notifiers, implementing the Status Notifier interface, fulfil different purposes. Examples include the archival of the alarm history in a database, the email notification of appropriate people about new alarms, and the display of the current alarm status on a web page.

The architecture is both flexible and extensible. It allows the use of multiple data sources, new alarm conditions via an alarms configuration file, and different notification mechanisms (e.g., SNMP traps).

As shown in Fig. 1 (by the shaded regions), the architecture conceptually consists of three main functional blocks: Query, Analysis and Status Notification. These functional blocks are discussed below. In order to help the discussion an analysis of the metrics necessary to monitor the alarms conditions and where to get the data for these metrics is presented. The NM-WG schema used is also discussed.

4.2 Metrics and Measurement Archives

In order to detect the alarm conditions it is necessary to monitor many different metrics; for example, route-changes, network link status, router packet drops and network link utilisation. These metrics are monitored by different tools and then made available through Measurement Archives (MAs). The Alarms Service has to be able to access the different MAs to obtain the required measurement data.

For instance, to monitor the Routing Alarm condition, it is necessary to obtain data about route-changes and network link status. The route-change information can be obtained from the perfSONAR Hades system [10]. Hades returns data based on traceroute measurements. However, to obtain information on the network link status it is necessary to access another MA; in this case the perfSONAR E2E Link Management system [11]. The E2E Link Management System supplies information on the status of an end-to-end network link by aggregating information from each segment of the path.

Similarly, to monitor the Interface Errors Alarm the Alarm Service requires data for router interface errors, whilst to monitor the Interface Congestion Alarm, data for router packet-drops and link utilisation are needed. This data can be accessed via a perfSONAR RRD MA [4], available as part of the perfSONAR MDM bundle. It is quite possible that each network administrative domain provides its own MA for its own routers; therefore the Alarms Service needs to be capable of accessing several different MAs simultaneously.

4.3 NM-WG Schema

As identified when discussing the motivation for this work, accessing different MAs is facilitated by the use of standard interfaces wherever possible, which in this case means interfaces following the schema defined by the OGF NM-WG [2]. These are XML schemas, which are defined for information such as the subject of a measurement (e.g., a network path or router interface), the metric measured (e.g., link utilisation or round-trip time), the time of a measurement, and the measurement data itself. The schemas are used by the Alarms Service to send a Request for particular measurement data, and then receive the corresponding Response containing the data, sent by an MA.

4.4 Query

Referring back to Fig. 1, one of the three main functional blocks of the architecture is the Query block, which is responsible for accessing various data sources and obtaining measurement data for metrics of interest. The Query block consists of an MA Query Interface (to "pull" data) and an MA Notification Interface (to "push" data).

The MA Query Interface uses the NM-WG schema to request and retrieve measurement data. More specifically, MA data is accessed via an NM-WG Web service interface. The use of this standard interface enables uniform access to heterogeneous MAs such as the perfSONAR RRD MA and perfSONAR Hades MA. Even though the data required by the current Alarms Service can be accessed via this NM-WG interface (since all necessary MAs provide such an interface) the architecture is flexible enough to add an MA query interface for non-NM-WG compliant data sources.

The MA Notification Interface is designed to allow the measurement data sources to push their data, or potentially aggregated measurements, to the Alarms Service. The idea behind this is that the Alarms Service a) does not need to pull data at regular intervals and b) can be used to combine pre-processed measurement data or even alarms from other systems.

4.5 Analysis

The components in the Analysis functional block form the Alarms Engine. The Alarms Engine consists of Pre-conditioner, Configuration Parser for rules, the Current Status Analyser and the Alarm Analyser. The engine is based on a user-configurable rules-based system. Rules provide a natural way to define alarms and are used in many different alerting systems (e.g., for monitoring values of shares in a stock market). Within the Alarms Service, they give flexibility in defining the conditions when an alarm should be raised. The user can define these conditions without using other programming skills, allowing them to be easily fine-tuned as part of routine maintenance. An *ad hoc* mechanism could have been used, but that would have "reinvented the wheel" and could have led to usability issues. The alarm rules are defined using the following structure:

```
rule "<rule name>"
  when
    <parameterised alarm condition>
  then
    <consequence>
end
```

An example of a rule specifying an Interface Congestion Alarm is shown below:

```
rule "Interface Congestion"
  when
    A router has output drops > "0" but utilisation is < "80" percent
  then
    Log : "Router has output drops"
    Raise InterfaceCongestionAlarm
end
```

The Alarms Engine triggers the querying of all configured MAs at user-defined intervals. It first constructs the query for each measurement subject and metric to be sent to the associated MA. After having retrieved the monitoring data for these via the NM-WG Web service interface, it then packs the data into internal data containers. The data in these containers is compared against the user-configured alarm rules within the Current Status Analyser. If the measurement data satisfies the condition of a rule, this rule gets activated and the associated data (subject, metric, alarm condition) is compiled and forwarded to the Alarm Analyser. The Alarm Analyser is designed to compare the raised alarm against the previous history of the subject in question, and to decide if the alarm should be raised via the Status Notification (see next section) or not. The Alarms Analyser resets an alarm if its condition is no longer there.

The separation between analysing the current status and the status history of a subject allows the detection of certain patterns, e.g. flapping between two states.

4.6 Status Notification

A status notification mechanism is provided to plug-in different notification methods. For example, status notifiers can be implemented to send emails, implement SNMP traps, write to web interfaces or integrate with a network weather-map system.

Concrete implementations of this interface register with the Alarm Analyser (described above). The interface provides three different types of notifications to declare if an alarm for a subject is "new", "updated" or "cleared". It is then up to the concrete notification implementation to process or ignore an alarm, depending on the type of notification.

5 An Implementation

The Alarms Service described above is implemented using the Java programming language. Java provides portability to different platforms and good performance.

The NM-WG requests and responses are implemented as described in [1]. The NM-WG client shown in the architecture uses Apache Axis2 to submit XML requests conforming to the NM-WG schema. Similarly, XML responses received are checked for compliance with the NM-WG schema prior to further processing.

The Alarms Engine uses Drools [12] to implement a rules-based system. The alarm rules specify which state of the measurement data containers resembles an alarm condition. However, this would lead to a low-level, programming-like configuration syntax, which would not be particularly user-friendly. Hence, the "Domain Specific Language" feature of the Drools library is used to create a more natural and user-friendly configuration language. This language is designed to read like a normal English sentence (e.g., A router has output drops > "0") and is automatically mapped to the actual internal rules code, lowering the learning curve for the configuration significantly.

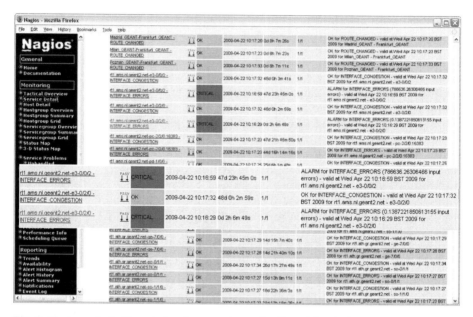

Fig. 2. Nagios web dashboard showing two alarms (replicated for clarity in the zoomed area) being raised (marked as "CRITICAL") for the GÉANT network

In order to help monitor the LHCOPN, an early version of the Alarms Service has been produced and released. This version is capable of monitoring the four alarm conditions described in this paper. It displays alarms on a Nagios-based [13] web dashboard (see Fig. 2). Email notifications can also be delivered via Nagios. Note that the Alarms service is an independent, Java application that is only loosely coupled with Nagios. This allows us to support in the future other web-based and notification mechanisms, as required.

Of the components in the architecture shown in Fig. 1, the pre-conditioner, the Alarms Archive, the Recent Status History and the MA Notification Interface have not been implemented yet. The pre-conditioner is delayed until there is a clear requirement for it. For example, whether "false positives" (i.e., an alarm being raised when there is no reason to do so, which may be due to a data anomaly) are noted in practice. See the deployment section for more on false positives. If Nagios is used as the web interface then the Alarms Archive is not required. This is because Nagios maintains its own alarms archive (Nagios refer to this as "Alert History"). The Recent Status History is also not implemented, as again Nagios maintains its own recent status. The Measurement Archive Notification Interface has not been implemented yet as none of the MAs currently used to supply data are capable of sending notifications – they all require active queries.

6 Deployment

The early version released [14] is currently deployed to monitor the first few Tier1 sites of the LHCOPN that currently supply monitoring data. More sites, including the Tier0 (CERN), will be added to the deployment of this Alarms Service as and when data become available from them. The deployment is carried out and maintained by the DANTE Service Desk. This version is successfully monitoring and raising relevant alarms for the configured network paths and router interfaces. So far no false positives have been noted from this deployment.

The same version of the Alarms Service has successfully been deployed by the authors at EPCC to monitor some of the networks for which data is publically available, for instance the GÉANT2 and GARR networks.

7 Conclusion and Future Work

This paper introduced an Alarms Service for monitoring multi-domain Grid networks. The service uses a flexible architecture to address the requirements gathered from the users and operators of such networks. The service uses an NM-WG standard interface to reduce the complexities of accessing monitoring data from heterogeneous sources. The service also uses a rules-based user configurable alarms definition mechanism. It is envisaged that with the adoption of the Alarms Service by underlying network infrastructures – such as the LHCOPN – large Grid infrastructures will benefit from smoother operations with timely troubleshooting.

At present, the Alarms Service has been deployed to monitor the LHCOPN. Projects such as GÉANT3 and DEISA2 [15] have noted an interest in the evaluation of the Alarms Service as part of their multi-domain network monitoring solution. Based on the deployments and interest, some of the unimplemented architectural components and other capabilities may get added to the Alarms Service.

Acknowledgments

We would like to thank: DANTE [6] for helping us with gathering requirements; LHCOPN [3] for contributing requirements and providing useful feedback following the various demonstrations of the software; and WiN-Labor [7] for help specifying the behaviour of the Alarm Service, providing prompt access to Hades and helping with MA-related issues.

This work has been funded by the UK Joint Information Systems Committee (JISC) and by the European Union under DEISA2 (RI-222919).

References

1. Kavoussanakis, K., Phipps, A., Palansuriya, C., Trew, A., Simpson, A., Baxter, R.: Federated network performance monitoring for the grid. In: 3rd International Conference on Broadband Communications, Networks, and Systems, San Jose, California, USA (2006)
2. Network Measurements Working Group, https://forge.gridforum.org/projects/nm-wg
3. Large Hadron Collider Optical Private Network (LHCOPN) TWiki, https://twiki.cern.ch/twiki/bin/view/LHCOPN/WebHome
4. PerfSONAR Services, http://www.perfsonar.net/services.html
5. Gurun, S., Szymanski, B.: Automatic Internet Routing Behaviour Analysis Using Public WWW Traceroute Service. Technical report, Department of Computer Science, University of California, Santa Barbara (2008)
6. DANTE, http://www.dante.net/server/show/nav.13
7. WiN-Labor, http://www.win-labor.dfn.de/German/mainpage.html
8. RFC2119, http://www.ietf.org/rfc/rfc2119.txt
9. Holleczek, T.: Statistical Analysis of IP Performance Metrics in International Research and Educational Networks. Master's Thesis, Department of Computer Science, Friedrich-Alexander-University Erlangen-Nuremberg (2008)
10. Hades MA Service, https://wiki.man.poznan.pl/perfsonar-mdm/index.php/Hades_MA_Service
11. PerfSONAR E2E Link Monitoring: System Design and Documentation, https://wiki.man.poznan.pl/perfsonar-mdm/images/perfsonar-mdm/1/12/GN2-JRA4-06-010v240.pdf
12. Drools, http://www.jboss.org/drools/
13. Nagios, http://www.nagios.org/
14. NPM Alarms Service, http://www.npm-alarms.org/
15. Distributed European Infrastructure for Supercomputing Applications, http://www.deisa.eu/

Grid Anywhere: An Architecture for Grid Computing Able to Explore the Computational Resources of the Set-Top Boxes

Fabiano Costa Teixeira, Marcos José Santana, Regina Helena Carlucci Santana, and Julio Cezar Estrella

Institute of Mathematics and Computer Science, University of São Paulo, São Carlos, Brazil
(teixeira,mjs,rcs,jcezar}@icmc.usp.br

Abstract. This paper shows a grid computing architecture called Grid Anywhere which aims at allowing the sharing of the computational resources from set-top boxes (receiver) of an Interactive Digital Television System. This sharing is made in a such a way that the TV broadcaster can use the set-top boxes tuned to it to get a high computational power and the user can also use remote resource of others devices (set-top boxes or personal computers) to increase the performance of the application executed in his receiver.

Keywords: Interactive Digital Television, Grid Computing, Peer-to-Peer networks.

1 Introduction

Brazil is a country which has a large number of TV devices, almost 54 millions [1]. In February 2, 2007 started in Brazil the transmissions of digital television signals. The reception of this signal and the audio/video reproduction are made by a device called set-top box.

The set-top box, in addition of the function cited in the previous paragraph, is able to execute applications which can be sent by the television signal broadcaster together with the audio and video streams. So, this device has computational resources, including cpu, memory and hard disk.

In the next years Brazil will have approximately 80 millions of digital receivers (set-top box) [11], then can be interesting the possibility of sharing computational resources hosted by this devices. This share can be made to offer a high performance execution environment. In addition, the user will be able to use remote resources hosted in other receivers or conventional personal computers to increase its computational power to execute applications. In this context this paper presents a proposal of a grid computing architecture that has as participants the conventional personal computers, interactive digital television signal broadcasters and set-top boxes. This document is organized as follows: the sections 2 and 3 show, respectively, a short introduction about Interactive Digital Television and grid computing paradigm. The section 4 shows the proposal of the architecture. The section 5 presents some object migration issues and section 6 shows a performance evaluation of object transfers using Java Sockets. Finally, the section 7 concludes the paper and presents some future works.

T. Doulamis et al.: (Eds.): GridNets 2009, LNICST 25, pp. 79–88, 2010.

2 Interactive Digital Television

In a digital television system many of the components are different from those found in an analogical one. Changes are found at the program production, transmission and reception of digital signal [2]. In figure 1, the production is made using a digital camera and the images are sent to a MPEG encoder which has the function of making the compression of data to be sent to the viewers (users). The data compression allows that a unique channel that today (in an analogical system) is able to transmit only one TV program can be used to transmit more than one simultaneously, depending of the video quality adopted.

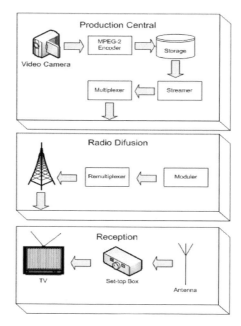

Fig. 1. Digital Television System Architecture. Based on [2].

The MPEG-2 Systems [3], technology used in the transport layer of the digital television system, allows that the audio, video and data streams can be multiplexed in a unique transport stream that is sent using the radio diffusion. An antenna has the function of receiving the signal propagated via broadcast and forward it to the set-top box.

The set-top box, device with computational resources (cpu, memory, operation system), in addition of its main functions (reception and decoding of the signal, reproduction of audio and video) is able to execute applications. Since a data stream can be transmitted, it can be used to transport an application (java application, for example) sent by the television broadcaster. So, this application can be received by the viewer's set-top box and executed.

Since the sent of the application is made via broadcast, when the set-top box is tuned in a channel the data stream transmission could be in curse. For audio and video streams it is not a problem. However, when an application has been transmitted, the receiver needs to get the whole file. The Data Carousel address this question: the data are divided in modules that are transmitted cyclically. So, if the initial modules have already been transmitted, the receiver waits for the retransmission of them [15].

The set-top boxes can be manufactured by various companies that, potentially can adopt different hardware and software solutions. So, in order to the same application sent by a television broadcaster could be executed in different types of receivers, as showed in figure 2, there is a software layer called middleware. The middleware has the function of providing transparency of hardware and software to the application. This transparency is achieved offering a generic API (application program interface).

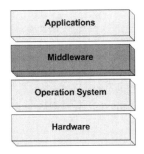

Fig. 2. Set-top Box's Layer Model. Based on [2].

In order to an application executed in the viewer's set-top box be able to send data to the television broadcaster or another entity, it is necessary a communication channel that has the function of allowing set-top box to access an IP network (Internet). This communication channel can be implemented using a lot of technologies like Wi-Max, ADSL, Cable [12].

3   Grid Computing

In 90's middle a new computing paradigm has been proposed to allow that computational resources geographically distributed and under independent administrations could be shared [4][5].

The resources to be shared can be since processors and disks to software licenses.

The possibility of sharing resources among users geographically distributed allows the building of a very powerful computational system, which can contribute in a significant way in the solution of problems, without using new hardware devices.

Institutions and individuals can be organized with the intention of sharing their resources. This group that determines a set of sharing rules and polices are called Virtual Organization (VO) [6].

Some projects of philanthropic computation have been using resources offered by voluntary users to contribute with the processing of larges information sets. Boinc Project is a framework that allows the building of this kind of application [7]. It hosts projects like SETI@home and Rosseta@home that work with processing of radio signal to look for intelligent extraterrestrial life and analyze of amino acid chains in the proteins formation, respectively.

Building a computational grid involves a lot of requirements. In order to abstract these requirements, the utilization of a middleware is very interesting. In this context, Globus Toolkit [8], an open source tool, was presented in 1998. Is gives a set of programs, services and libraries that aim the construction of a grid computing providing mechanisms for security, resource management, application submission and data transfer.

A Brazilian product called OURGRID [9] also gives facilities to build a grid computing. However, the system developed uses peer-to-peer architecture and the tasks are submitted using a BoT (Bag of Tasks) approach. So, the applications can't communicate with each other.

A middleware called DGET (Data Grid Environment and Tools) [10], using Java objects migration, allows the construction of a grid computing.

The work proposed in [11] describes a grid computing architecture called TVGrid, which uses the idle computational resources found in a set-top box. This approach is based on the transmission of the application via broadcast to be executed in the viewer receiver. These applications are executed and the results are sent back to the broadcaster.

4 Grid Anywhere Architecture

Nowadays, Brazil has a large number of TV devices, approximately 54 millions [1] and potentially in 2017 the country will have almost 80 millions of set-top boxes [11].

Since each set-top box is composed by computational resources, in a near future a big computational park will be found in Brazil and lots of these resources could be idle in some periods of time.

The architecture proposed in this paper aims the construction of a grid computing using conventional personal computers and set-top boxes. However, the proposal has a bidirectional approach where a set-top box could act in two roles: resource provider and resource consumer.

When a receiver acts as a resource provider, a complex application could be divided in short parts to be sent, by the television broadcaster, in order to be executed by the set-top boxes. When the processing finish, the results are sent back via a communication channel. Acting as a resource consumer, a limited set-top box can use idle computational resources found in others receivers or conventional personal computers to increase its computational power to execute applications.

To build this grid computing, peer-to-peer architecture has been used, supposing that the receivers used in Brazil will have a communication channel that alows a direct communication between the set-top boxes. So, as presented in figure 3, each set-top box (TV Peer), personal computer (PC Peer) and TV broadcaster (Broadcaster Peer) represents a node of this network.

The resource sharing is made using Java object migration between the participants. Therefore, an object can be exported to another peer, its methods can be remotely invoked and the result or the object come back to the original peer.

The PC Peer is a participant that can either contact or be contacted by any other participant under a peer-to-peer connection to migrate the Java objects to be executed.

The Broadcaster Peer represents a high computational power entity, since it can receive a Java object and send it via broadcast to all set-top boxes tuned to it.

Finally, the TV Peer is the participant that has all PC Peer's characteristics. However, it is able to receive Java Objects sent via broadcast by Broadcaster Peer.

Since the viewers need to share their set-top box, this proposal hopes that will be some business model that incentives them to enable the set-top boxes to be used to execute applications sent by the broadcaster.

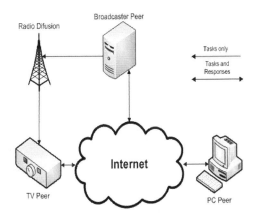

Fig. 3. Grid computing architecture

4.1 Middleware

This proposal includes a middleware architecture that is instaled in the peer, which can be either a PC, a TV Broadcaster or a set-top box.

The Grid Anywhere Middleware aims at offering to the application programmer an environment to build grid applications in a transparent way. Since the grid is based on Java objects migration and remote method invocation, a programming model where the programmer defines the classes that can be accessed remotely has been adopted. The middleware, using code instrumentation [13], automatically manages the migration and remote method invocation. So, the user doesn't needs to worry about the details of the process.

As showed in figure 4, the middleware has a core API that can be invoked in two ways in order to get advanced information about the grid and to take actions: explicitly by expert programmers or by instrumented java code.

The *scheduler,* when required, analyzes the grid environment to find the best peer to send a serialized object to be hosted there and executed. The programmer needs to define if the object requests either a single host (so, it can be sent to a PC Peer or a TV Peer in a unicast mode) or a high performance host. The second case is indicated when there is a large data set that can be processed by a same algorithm. So, the object which implements that algorithm can be sent to a Broadcaster Peer which sends

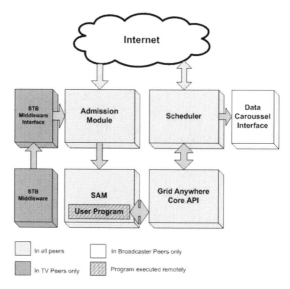

Fig. 4. Grid Anywhere middleware architecture

this object to every set-top box tuned to it. The set-top box receives the object and executes it. The Java program executed can use conventional communications interfaces (like sockets) or the middleware API to get the data to be processed. When the processing has been done, the results are sent back to the original peer.

The *admission control* module is used when the peer is in the role of resource provider. It negotiates the execution with the client *scheduler* and receives a Java Object to be hosted in the local peer. Since the object has been received, in order to give security guarantees to the resource provider, the Java Object is sent to be executed in the SAM module (a sand box responsible to execute the applications in a secure way).

When the resource provider is a TV Peer, the reception of Java Objects sent by the Broadcaster is made by the set-top box middleware. So, there is a *set-top box middleware interface* module that is responsible to get the received object and forward it to the admission module. In this first work, an interface to Ginga (the Brazilian Middleware) will be implemented. In order to integrate the Grid Anywhere to another Interactive Digital Television System, it is possible to implement the set-top box middleware interface, what makes the middleware flexible.

In situations where there is no set-top box middleware, it is necessary to implement programs to manage the incoming data carousel. In future work, this module will be implemented to give "independency" to the Grid Anywhere middleware.

The Broadcaster Peer uses the Data Carousel Interface to forward the Java Object to the Broadcaster's application responsible for multiplexing data with audio and video to be sent to the viewer receivers (set-top boxes).

4.2 Security

The security is a very important issue in the Grid Environment implemented by the proposal presented in this paper. The peers execute programs in most times implemented by unknown programmers. So, the program execution in an insecurity mode can be very dangerous to the local system.

The SAM is a sand-box responsible to execute Java program in a secure way. To do it the user program is executed over a *Java Security Manager* and an *Environment Monitor*, and both over a *Police System*, as show in figure 5.

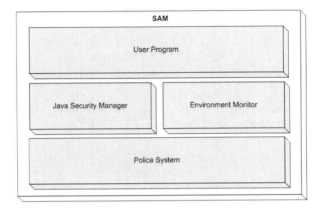

Fig. 5. SAM layered model architecture

The *Police System* is a set of rules defined by the user, which defines what a program can do(open files, sockets) and the amount of resources that can be used (memory, cpu, bandwidth). The Java Security Manager and the Environment Monitor are responsible to make these controls respectively.

The Java Security Manager used in this architecture is an override of the original one distributed with JRE. Instead of using the Access Controller [14] to define the access rules, the SAM implementation uses an own Police System to enable that more flexible rules can be defined.

Middleware users can define the rules based in the concept of user groups, subgroups and users. In a Grid Computing environment, the group entity can be mapped to a Virtual Organization (VO). So, in a trusted VO the access rights can be more than in an untrusted one. In addition, other rules types can be established, giving a high flexibility to define the security polices.

Since the middleware aims at giving an easier tool which could be used by users without experience in computing, the interfaces used to configure it need to be very simple. In a Interactive Digital Television System context, the user need to be able to configure the polices using the TV's remote control. So, the SAM has a friendly and intuitive graphical tool to define the security rules.

5   Object Migration

Since our approach aims at increasing the processing throughput and decrease the response time (when an interactive application is used), the Grid Anywhere middleware is based on Java objects migration. Every time that a grid peer needs to get more computational power to execute its application, some objects are serialized and sent to another peer (which rebuild the object). A XML document is used to describe the method invocation (method name and parameters values). When the processing is done three actions are possible: a) the value returned from the method is sent to the caller; b) if a *void* method is called, the object still at the destination host with a possible state change; c) the object is serialized again and returned to the caller. Figure 6 shows a sequence diagram that presents the message pattern exchange (MEP) of Grid Anywhere.

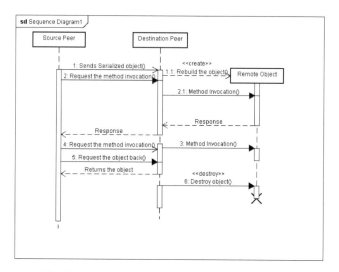

Fig. 6. Message pattern exchange for Grid Anywhere

The sequence 1 explains a synchronous invocation, whereas sequence 4 shows an asynchronous invocation (without response). Finally, the sequence 5 presents a process to request the object back.

To do the object transfer our middleware uses Java Sockets. It is important to consider the object's size before migration because of the transfer overhead. The scheduler could make a time prediction that will be spent to migrate an object and take the decision of either move the object (and to decide the destination peer) or keep it locally. In order to verify if the time prediction is possible, a performance evaluation has done and presented in the next section.

6 Test Environment

In order to verify if scheduler could make a transfer's overhead prediction, an initial experiment has been done. Using two computers geographically separated and two cable modems, data sets with different sizes (from 1KB to 20KB) was transmitted between the machines. The same data set was transmitted ten times using the API Java Sockets and the time spent was stored in order to calculate the time average, standard deviation and confidence interval for each data size.

Figure 7 shows the transfer behaviors when a cable modem has been used.

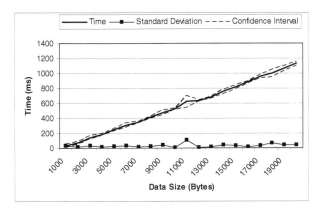

Fig. 7. Behavior of transfers using cable

When the cable technology was used the transfer's time has increased in a linear way (in function of object's size). With a discrete standard deviation and a short confidential interval, a mathematical function could be implemented in order to compute the transfer's time for a given Java object. Therefore, time predictions could be done, in some cases, with a minimal insurance. However, other link technologies could present different behaviors.

A mechanism to determine, in execution time, if a transfer's overhead prediction could be done in function of the data link used by the peer is been created.

7 Conclusion

In Brazil there is a large number of TV devices and the popularization of the internet could create a big computational park composed by resources of the set-top boxes.

Grid Anywhere, the architecture proposed in this paper, enables the construction of a grid computing able to use the idle resources of the set-top boxes in the processing of complex applications. This can be very useful to the general engineering and science since a high computational power could be found in a architecture with a high number of set-top boxes using the middleware.

Since the Grid Anywhere also allows that the set-top box uses the remote idle resources found in other receivers or personal computers to increase its computational power, the architecture can contribute to the digital inclusion in Brazil enabling that viewers with limited financial resources could execute more complex application.

Actually, a prototype of the security and object migration modules has been implemented. In future work the interfaces with the set-top box middleware and data carousel generator will be constructed in order to allow a performance evaluation of the object migration in a Interactive Digital Television System.

References

1. Zuffo, M.K.: TV Digital Aberta no Brasil – Políticas Estruturais para um Modelo Nacional. Escola Politécnica, USP, São Paulo (2003)
2. Fernandes, J., Lemos, G., Silveira, G.: Introdução à Televisão Digital Interativa: Arquitetura, Protocolos, Padrões e Práticas. Jornada de Atualização em Informática do Congresso da Sociedade Brasileira de Computação (2004)
3. Sarginson, P.A.: MPEG-2: A Tutorial Introduction to the System Layer. In: IEE Colloquium on MPEG-2: What it is and what it isn't (1995)
4. Foster, I.: The Grid: A New Infrastructure for 21st Century Science. Physics Today 55, 42–47 (2002)
5. Teixeira, F.C., Toledo, M.B.F.: Arquitetura de Grade Computacional Baseada em Modelos Econômicos. I2TS, Cuiabá, Brasil (2006)
6. Foster, I., Kesselman, C., Tuecke, S.: The Anatomy of the Grid: Enabling Scalable Virtual Organizations. International Journal of Supercomputer Applications 15, 200–222 (2001)
7. Boinc Home Page. Disponível em, http://boinc.berkeley.edu
8. Foster, I.: Globus Toolkit Version 4: Software for Service-Oriented Systems. In: Jin, H., Reed, D., Jiang, W. (eds.) NPC 2005. LNCS, vol. 3779, pp. 2–13. Springer, Heidelberg (2005)
9. Andrade, N., Costa, L., Germóglio, G., Cirne, W.: Peer-to-Peer grid computing with the OurGrid Community. SBRC, Fortaleza-CE (2005)
10. Hudzia, B., Ellahi, T.N., McDermott, L., Kechadi, T.: A Java Based Architecture of P2P-Grid Middleware, Arxiv preprint cs.DC/0608113 (2006)
11. Batista, C.E.C.F., Araujo, T.M.U., Omaia, D., Anjos, T.C., Castro, G.M.L., Brasileiro, F.V., Souza Filho, G.L.: TVGrid: A Grid Architecture to use the idle resources on a Digital TV network. In: Proceedings of the Seventh IEEE International Symposium on Cluster Computing and the Grid, pp. 823–828 (2007)
12. Farias, M.C.Q., Carvalho, M.M., Alencar, M.S.: Digital Television Broadcasting in Brazil. IEEE Multimedia 15(2), 64–70 (2008)
13. Chiba, S., Nishizawa, M.: An Easy-to-Use Toolkit for Efficient Java Bytecode Translators. In: Pfenning, F., Smaragdakis, Y. (eds.) GPCE 2003. LNCS, vol. 2830, pp. 364–376. Springer, Heidelberg (2003)
14. Java Security Architecture, http://java.sun.com/j2se/1.4.2/docs/guide/security/spec/security-specTOC.fm.html
15. Herpel, C.: Elementary Stream Management in MPEG-4. IEEE Transactions on Circuits and Systems for Video Technology 9, 315–324 (2002)

The Open Cloud Testbed: Supporting Open Source Cloud Computing Systems Based on Large Scale High Performance, Dynamic Network Services

Robert Grossman[1, 2], Yunhong Gu[1], Michal Sabala[1], Colin Bennet[2], Jonathan Seidman[2], and Joe Mambratti[3]

[1] National Center for Data Mining, University of Illinois at Chicago
[2] Open Data Group
[3] International Center for Advanced Internet Research, Northwestern University

Abstract. Recently, a number of cloud platforms and services have been developed for data intensive computing, including Hadoop, Sector, CloudStore (formerly KFS), HBase, and Thrift. In order to benchmark the performance of these systems, to investigate their interoperability, and to experiment with new services based on flexible compute node and network provisioning capabilities, we have designed and implemented a large scale testbed called the Open Cloud Testbed (OCT). Currently OCT has 120 nodes in 4 data centers: Baltimore, Chicago (two locations), and San Diego. In contrast to other cloud testbeds, which are in small geographic areas and which are based on commodity Internet services, the OCT is a wide area testbed and the 4 data centers are connected with a high performance 10Gb/s network, based on a foundation of dedicated lightpaths. This testbed can address the requirements of extremely large data streams that challenge other types of distributed infrastructure. We have also developed several utilities to support the development of cloud computing systems and services, including novel node and network provisioning services, a monitoring system, and an RPC system. In this paper, we describe the OCT concepts, architecture, infrastructure, a few benchmarks that were developed for this platform, interoperability studies, and results.

1 Introduction

Cloud computing has become quite popular during the last few years, in part because it provides a practical solution to multiple types of application requirements. First, the popular cloud computing services are very easy to use. Users can request computing resources on demand from cloud service providers. Also, most users find the Hadoop Distributed File System (HDFS) and the Hadoop implementation of MapReduce [8] very easy to use compared to traditional high performance computing programming frameworks, such as MPI. Second, basic cloud facilities can be readily deployed. The basic unit consists of racks of standard compute servers. Third, the payment model provides advantages to communities with variable resource requirements. For example, it allows for quick implementation of processing resources without an upfront capital investment.

T. Doulamis et al.: (Eds.): GridNets 2009, LNICST 25, pp. 89–97, 2010.
© Institute for Computer Sciences, Social-Informatics and Telecommunications Engineering 2010

Basically, there are three types of cloud software systems (Figure 1): 1) the low level resource manager and provider (Amazon EC2 [5], Eucalyptus [4]), which has been called Infrastructure as a Service or IaaS; 2) distributed storage and data processing services such as those provided by Hadoop [2], CloudStore [3], and Sector/Sphere [1] that can be used to build data intensive applications (Platform as a Service or PaaS); and 3) domain specific software, or Software as a Service (SaaS) such as Google Docs.

As the number of different cloud services grows, it has become clear that potential users can benefit from an environment that could be used for benchmarking different systems and testing their interoperability. The Open Cloud Testbed (OCT) was designed to benchmark cloud systems, to investigate their interoperability, and to experiment with implementations on novel infrastructure, such as large scale high performance optical networks. Also, networks are integrated as "first class" controllable,

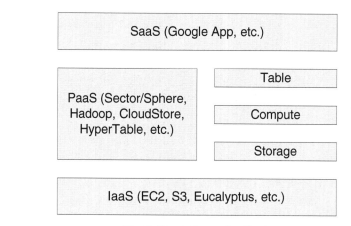

Fig. 1. Cloud Computing Stack

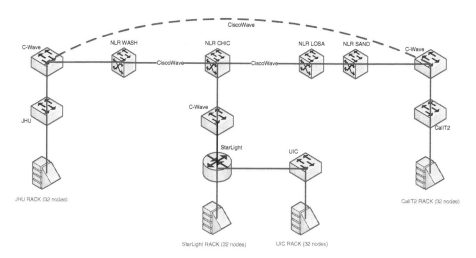

Fig. 2. The Open Cloud Testbed System Diagram

adjustable resources not merely as external resources. We have installed and tested Eucalyptus, Hadoop, CloudStore (KosmosFS), Sector/Sphere, and Thrift with various applications.

In addition, we have also developed network libraries, monitoring systems, and benchmark suites to support the development and experimental studies of cloud computing stacks.

In this paper, we introduce the OCT concept, architecture, infrastructure, the software we built to utilize the testbed, the experimental studies we conducted with various cloud software, and preliminary results of those studies.

2 The Open Cloud Testbed

2.1 Concepts and Objectives

The OCT architecture envisions the emergence of powerful large scale applications supported by services and processes based on highly distributed, integrated facilities and infrastructure. This infrastructure is an extremely flexible programmable platform that enables new functions and capabilities to easily be created and implemented. OCT represents a departure from existing clouds is several ways. For example, as its name implies, it is based on a concept of interoperability and openness. Also, traditional clouds use fairly generic common components and protocols across their services and infrastructure. The OCT architecture incorporates high performance services, protocols, and infrastructure at all levels. Instead of using the commodity Internet, it uses a national high performance 10 Gb/s network based on extremely fast transport protocols supported by dedicated light paths. Although such capabilities are fairly rare today, this approach is being used to model future distributed infrastructure, which will provide much more capacity and capabilities than current systems. For example, as commonly implemented, clouds do not support large data streams well. In contrast, OCT is being designed not only to manage millions of small streams and small amounts of information but also extremely large data sets.

The objectives of the OCT initiative extend beyond creative novel high performance capabilities. Another important research objective is to develop standards and frameworks for interoperating between different cloud software. Currently, we have tested Eucalyptus, CloudStore (formerly KosmosFS), Hadoop, Sector/Sphere, and Thrift. In particular, we developed an interface so that Hadoop can use Sector as its storage system.

2.2 The OCT Infrastructure

As illustrated in Figure 2, currently there are 4 racks of servers in OCT, located in 4 data centers at Johns Hopkins University (Baltimore), StarLight (Chicago), the University of Illinois (Chicago), and the University of California (San Diego). Each rack has 32 nodes. Each node has dual dual-core AMD 2.4GHz CPU, 12GB memory, 1TB single SATA disk, and dual 1GE NICs. Two Cisco 3750E switches connect the 32 nodes, which then connects to the outside by a 10Gb/s uplink.

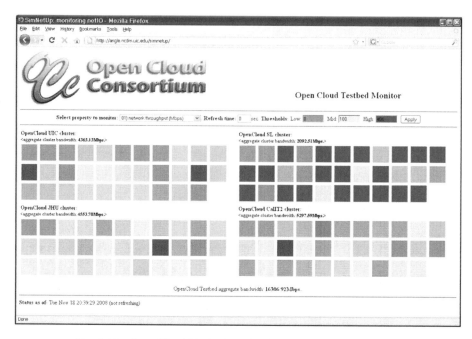

Fig. 3. The Open Cloud Testbed monitoring and visualization system

In contrast to other testbeds, the OCT utilizes wide area high performance networks, not the familiar commodity Internet. There is 10Gb/s connection (provided by the CiscoWave national testbed infrastructure, which spans the US east, west, north and south) between any two data centers. The majority of experimental studies we perform extend over all four geographically distributed racks. Almost all other cloud testbeds operate each data center locally and independently.

We are currently installing two more racks (60 nodes) and expect to install two additional racks by the end of 2009. By then the OCT will have about 250 nodes and 1000 cores. We will also extend the 10GE network to MIT Lincoln Lab (Cambridge) and Pittsburgh Supercompter Center/Carnegie Mellon University (Pittsburgh).

3 Monitoring and Visualization

When using distributed resources, managing and monitoring the OCT requires substantial time as the testbed grows larger. Management costs can increase sharply as the number of sites increases. To mitigate this effect, we have developed a simple but effective monitoring and real time visualization system to track the behavior of every node in the OCT [11]. The OCT monitoring system reads the resource utilization (including CPU, memory, disk, NIC, etc.) on each node and a web-based visualization allows us to easily and directly monitor the entire system.

In addition, the monitoring system also helps with benchmarking and debugging cloud software. The visualization effectively indicates the real time status of the testbed (for example, if it is fully utilized and if the load is balanced across the test-bed). This capability has proved invaluable when debugging cloud services.

A snapshot of the web-based visualization can be found in Figure 3. Each block represents a server node, while each group of blocks represent a cluster. The color of each block represents the usage of a particular resource, in this case, network IO throughput. Color on the green/light side means the machine is idle; color on the red/dark side means the machine is busy.

In the Sector/Sphere software, we also have built-in a monitoring system that is used to improve load balancing and to remove nodes and/or network segments that exhibit poor performance. While the OCT monitoring system reads per node information, the built-in monitoring system of Sector reads the resource usage of the Sector process on each node and the network utilization based on the topology.

Sector assumes that the underlying network has a hierarchical topology, such as the one used by OCT. Based on this topology, Sector computes the aggregate network throughput on each link, in addition to each node. This process helps to identity a malfunctioning link or node and Sector can therefore remove such underperforming resources from the system.

The OCT architecture is based on an assumption that services are based on flexible, not static, foundation resources. The architecture provides for continuous monitoring of conditions, analysis, and dynamic change, including at the level of network resources. OCT leverages and builds on recent research and development trends in architecture and technologies that provide for dynamically provisioned network resources [13]. Using such capabilities for OCT implementations demonstrates the importance of designing dynamic vs. static network resources.

4 GMP: A Messaging Protocol

We have also designed and developed a unique high performance messaging protocol called GMP (Group Messaging Protocol) for Sector and other distributed systems. GMP allows an application to send a message quickly and reliably to another node. High performance messaging is essential for rapid reconfigurations of core resources under changing conditions. The protocol is suitable for delivering small control messages in distributed systems.

GMP is a connection-less protocol, which uses a single UDP port and which can send messages to any GMP instances or receive messages from other GMP instances. Because there is no connection setup required, GMP is much faster than TCP, which requires a connection set up between the involved nodes. On the other hand, UDP is unreliable. GMP, which is built on top of UDP, does not have any virtual connection, but maintains a list of states for each peer addresses to which it sends messages or from which it receives messages.

Every GMP message contains a session ID and a sequence number. Upon receiving a message, GMP sends back an acknowledgment; if no acknowledgment is received, the message will be sent again. The sequence number is used to make sure that no duplicated message will be delivered. The session ID is used to differentiate messages from the same address but different processes (e.g., if one process is restarted it will use a different session ID). If the message size is greater than a single UDP packet can hold, GMP will set up a UDT [12] connection to deliver the large message. However, we expect such a situation to be rare for GMP.

In Sector, we also developed a light-weight high performance RPC mechanism on top of GMP. The RPC library simply sends out a request in a GMP message and then it waits for the response to come back.

5 Benchmarks

We developed various standard benchmark applications to evaluate cloud software. Certain benchmarks designed previously for other systems, such as Terasort, have also been adopted.

In this section we described a benchmark called MalStone [14], which is specially designed to evaluate the ability of cloud systems in the support of distributed data intensive applications.

MalStone is a stylized analytic computation that requires the analysis of log files containing events about computers (entities) visiting web sites of the following form:

| Event ID | Timestamp | Site ID | Compromise Flag | Entity ID

The assumption is that some of the entities that visit certain web sites become compromised. In order to find out the bad sites that compromise computers, the benchmark application requires that a ratio be computed *for each site* that for a specified time window measures the percent of entities that become compromised at any time in the window.

Two sub-tasks are formed. MalStone-A computes the overall ratio per site. Malstone-B computes a series of windows-based ratio per site.

This type of computation requires only a few lines of code if the data is on a single machine (and can be done easily in a database). On the other hand, if the data is distributed over the nodes in a cloud, then we have found this type of computation turns out to be a useful benchmark for comparing different storage and compute services.

An example of a situation that might result in these types of log files is what are sometimes termed drive-by exploits [10]. These incidents result when users visit web sites containing code that can infect and compromise vulnerable systems. Not all visitors become infected but some do.

We have also developed a data generator for the MalStone benchmark called MalGen.

6 Experimental Studies

In this section, we describe several experimental studies we currently conduct on OCT.

In the first series of experiments, we used MalGen to generate 500 million 100-byte records on 20 nodes (for a total of 10 billion records or 1 TB of data) in the Open Cloud Testbed and compared the MalStone performance using: 1) the Hadoop Distributed File System (HDFS) with Hadoop's implementation of MapReduce; 2) the Hadoop HDFS with Streams and MalStone coded in Python; and, 3) the Sector Distributed File System and MalStone coded in Sector's User Defined Functions (UDF). The results are below (Table 1):

Table 1. Hadoop version 0.18.3 and Sector version 1.20 were used for these tests. Times are expressed in minutes (m) and seconds (s).

	Malstone-A	MalStone-B
Hadoop MapReduce	454m 13s	840m 50s
Hadoop Streams with Python	87m 29s	142m 32s
Sector/Sphere	33m 40s	43m 44s

Sector/Sphere benefit significantly from its data movement optimization (bandwidth load balancing and UDT data transfer) and it performs much faster than Hadoop.

We have conducted extensive experimental studies with different versions of Sector and Hadoop. The benchmark applications include distributed sorting and MalStone.

Table 2. This table compares the performance of Hadoop and Sector for a computation performed in one location using 28 nodes and 4 locations using 7 nodes each

	28 Local Nodes	7 * 4 Distributed Nodes	Wide Area Penalty
Hadoop (3 replicas)	8650	11600	34%
Hadoop (1 replica)	7300	9600	31%
Sector	4200	4400	4.7%

In the second series of experiments, we used MalGen to 15 billion on 28 nodes in one location and compared these results to the same computation performed when the nodes where distributed over four locations in the testbed. See Table 2. The experiment shows the impact of wide area networks on the performance of such applications. The performance penalty on Hadoop is 31~34%, while Sector suffers a 4.7% performance drop.

There are two major reasons for the better performance of Sector over wide area networks. First, Sector employs a load balancing mechanism to smoothly distribute the network traffic within the system. Second, Sector uses UDT [12] for data transfer. UDT is a high performance protocol that performs significantly better than TCP over wide area networks. The limitations of TCP are well documented [13].

7   Related Testbeds

There are several other testbeds that serve similar or related goals as that of OCT. The most closely related one in the Open Cirrus Testbed [9]. Open Cirrus consists of 6 sites with various number of nodes between 128 and 480 per site. While Open Cirrus contains more nodes than OCT, there is no data exchange between any two Open Cirrus sites. That is, Open Cirrus is designed for systems that run in a single data center.

Another cloud computing testbed is the Google-IBM testbed, which is similar to Open Cirrus, but it is smaller in scale.

Amazon's EC2 provides an economical alternative for certain cloud computing research. However, in EC2 users cannot control data locality and network configuration, thus it limits the value of related system research. In addition, while EC2 is inexpensive for temporary use, it actually poses a higher expense for long term system research purpose.

Other computing testbeds such as the TeraGrid were designed for mostly application research. Their usage on cloud computing system research were very limited.

8 Conclusion

Cloud computing has proven to be an important resource for many types of applications, from those oriented to consumers to those focused on the enterprise to those that support large scale science. This trend is expected to continue to the foreseeable future. However, more progress is required to fully utilize the cloud model. The OCT initiative was established in order to advance the state of cloud architecture and implementations. By benchmarking the performance of existing systems, investigating their interoperability, and experimenting with new services based on flexible compute node and network provisioning capabilities, more of the potential promised by the cloud model can be realized. Therefore, we have created and conducted experiments on the Open Cloud Testbed (OCT) a wide area testbed, based on a foundation of dedicated lightpaths. This testbed was used to investigate multiple services, protocols, processes and components, including novel node and network provisioning services, a monitoring system, and an RPC system. The results are extremely promising, and they indicate that the concepts described here are an important direction for additional research projects. Also, we believe that OCT is an important step to standardize cloud computing software and it is also a unique platform to benchmark the performance and interoperability of different clouds. By building on the concepts presented here, it may be possible to achieve significant advances in the development of next generation clouds over the next few years.

References

[1] Gu, Y., Grossman, R.: Sector and Sphere: The Design and Implementation of a High Performance Data Cloud. Theme Issue of the Philosophical Transactions of the Royal Society A: Crossing Boundaries: Computational Science, E-Science and Global E-Infrastructure 367(1897), 2429–2445 (2009)
[2] Hadoop, http://hadoop.apache.org/core/
[3] CloudStore, http://kosmosfs.sourceforge.net/

[4] Nurmi, D., Wolski, R., Grzegorczyk, C., Obertelli, G., Soman, S., Youseff, L., Zagorod-nov, D.: The Eucalyptus Open-source Cloud-computing System. In: Proceedings of Cloud Computing and Its Applications, Chicago, Illinois (October 2008)

[5] Amazon EC2 and S3, http://aws.amazon.com/

[6] Thrift, http://developers.facebook.com/thrift/

[7] Ghemawat, S., Gobioff, H., Leung, S.-T.: The Google File System, pub. In: 19th ACM Symposium on Operating Systems Principles, Lake George, NY (October 2003)

[8] Dean, J., Ghemawat, S.: MapReduce: Simplified Data Processing on Large Clusters. In: OSDI 2004: Sixth Symposium on Operating System Design and Implementation, San Francisco, CA (December 2004)

[9] HP Technical Report, HP-2009-122: Open Cirrus Cloud Computing Testbed: Federated Data Centers for Open Source Systems and Services Research

[10] Provos, N., McNamee, D., Mavrommatis, P., Wang, K., Modadugu, N.: The Ghost In The Browser - Analysis of Web-based Malware. In: Proceedings of the First Workshop on Hot Topics in Understanding Botnets, HotBots (2007)

[11] OCT Monitor, http://angle.ncdm.uic.edu/simnetup/

[12] Gu, Y., Grossman, R.L.: UDT: UDP-based Data Transfer for High-Speed Wide Area Networks. Computer Networks 51(7) (May 2007)

[13] Travestino, F., Mambretti, J., Karmous-Edwards, G.: GridNetworks: Enabling Grids With Advanced Communication Services. Wiley, Chichester (2006)

[14] Bennett, C., Grossman, R., Seidman, J.: Open Cloud Consortium Technical Report TR-09-01, MalStone: A Benchmark for Data Intensive Computing (April 2009)

Green Grids Workshop

Designing Power-Efficient WDM Ring Networks

Isabella Cerutti*, Luca Valcarenghi, and Piero Castoldi

Scuola Superiore Sant'Anna, Pisa, Italy
{isabella.cerutti,luca.valcarenghi,piero.castoldi}@sssup.it

Abstract. Traditionally, optical networks have been designed with the objective of minimizing the capital expenditure (CAPEX) without considering the operative costs (OPEX), due for instance to energy consumption. However, the increase of energy consumption and corresponding costs and the challenges imposed by the environmental issues (such as the global warming and the limited oil reserves) are demanding for a more responsible energy usage, including in the optical networking field.

The paper discusses how the mandate of saving energy can be included into the network design process. Power-saving design of WDM metro rings with traffic grooming capabilities is presented and compared against CAPEX-optimized designs. Considerations on the power efficiency and cost efficiency of different ring architectures are derived.

Keywords: optical network design, traffic grooming, power saving, unidirectional WDM ring.

1 Introduction

Metro networks require a careful planning in order to aggregate the traffic of the different types of services (e.g., grid services, voice) and to reduce the costs. In the past years, planning of optical network has always aimed at selecting the minimum amount of resources to support the requested traffic demands, i.e., at minimizing the equipment and installation costs, also known as capital expenditures (CAPEX). Operative costs (OPEX) – in particular the costs for powering the optical and electronic equipment – have been always overlooked and considered marginal by network providers. However, a reconsideration of the validity of these assumptions is required for the increase of energy costs [1, 11] and for environmental issues [9].

Pioneering studies on the evaluation of the energy consumption of optical network equipment were carried out by Tucker and Butler. Their works include thorough studies on the power consumption of optical and electronic switching systems [2, 12] and the comparison between different technologies [13]. Subsequent works have focused on IP routers [6, 7], and discussed power consumption

---

* The work described in this paper was carried out with the support of the BONE-project ("Building the Future Optical Network in Europe"), a Network of Excellence funded by the European Commission through the 7th ICT-Framework Programme.

T. Doulamis et al.: (Eds.): GridNets 2009, LNICST 25, pp. 101–108, 2010.

issues and possible savings. However, these initial works are restricted to single systems (i.e., node) or few interconnected systems. Subsequent studies have considered the power consumption of all-optical networks [3, 8] and multi-layer optical networks [3, 5, 10] and provided precious considerations on how to improve the network power efficiency.

In this paper, the power consumption is accounted during the design of WDM metro networks with unidirectional ring topology. Three architectural designs with different degrees of optical transparency and traffic grooming capabilities are considered [4]. In the first generation (FG) architecture, every node electronically processes and aggregates all the incoming connection traffic, including the in-transit traffic. In the single hop (SH) architecture, every node electronically processes only traffic that is inserted into or extracted from the network at that node, i.e., wavelength connections, or lightpaths, bypass transparently the intermediate optical nodes. The (hybrid) multi-hop (MH) architecture makes use of both lightpaths and electronic traffic grooming that is performed at few selected intermediate nodes.

The paper presents a model that quantifies the network power consumption at the optical layer, at the electronic layer and at their interfaces. Such model is included into the design of the three architectures. The main objective of the work is to address the open questions about 1) whether the design of a network at minimum CAPEX is equivalent to a design at minimum OPEX (i.e., power consumption), and 2) whether the CAPEX-efficient architectures are also OPEX-efficient.

To address these open questions, the design of a unidirectional WDM ring, based on either a FG, SH, or MH architecture, is OPEX-optimized and compared against the CAPEX-optimized design, for increasing rate of the traffic demands and various scenarios of power consumption in the optical and electronic layers. The comparison between CAPEX-optimized and OPEX-optimized designs and among the different architectural designs will help to derive useful considerations on designing power-efficient WDM rings.

2   Power Budget Model

To operate a multi-layer optical network, power needs to be supplied to each layer (i.e., the optical layer and the electronic layer) and to the interface between the two layers (i.e., for electrical-optical and optical-electrical conversion). At the different layers and at their interfaces, a number of factors influence the power consumption and the most relevant are: the emploied technology, the design of the systems, and the operating conditions. In order to derive a power budget model, a brief discussion on the three different contributions to the power consumption and on the made assumptions is carried out next.

2.1   Powering the E/O and O/E Interfaces

Electrical-optical (E/O) and optical-electrical (O/E) interfaces are transmitters and receivers, that, respectively, convert the electronic signal into optical signal

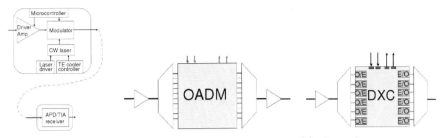

(a) Transmitter and (b) Optical add-drop multiplexer (c) Digital cross-connect
receiver architecture   (OADM) architecture   (DXC) architecture

Fig. 1. Network equipment for the E/O and O/E interfaces (a), at the optical layer
(b), and at the electrical layer (c)

and vice-versa. Usually, transmitters (Fig. 1(a)) consist of a laser, a modulator,
a laser driver, and a thermo-electric (TE) cooler. While power efficiency of a
laser is typically very high (i.e., the power consumption is as the one at the
optical layer), the modulator and the laser driver may drain the most of the
power within the transmitter [2]. The receivers (Fig. 1(a)) consist of a photo-
diode followed by a trans-impedence amplifier (TIA), whose power consumption
is non-negligible.

Since a transmitter and a receiver is required for each lightpath to be established, the overall power drained by the various components of the transmitters
and receivers can be accounted on a per-lightpath basis.

2.2   Powering the Optical Layer

The optical signal transmission is affected by power losses and by linear and non-
linear impairments. Power losses decreases exponentially the transmitted power
in function of the distance, making the signal amplification or regeneration necessary. The power consumed by the amplifiers is accounted by assuming that amplifiers are required and present at the nodes operating at the optical layer. In the
following, the impact of linear and non-linear physical impairments is neglected[1].

The optical signal bypasses transparently the nodes operating at the optical
layer, i.e., the nodes equipped with an add-drop multiplexer (OADM) (Fig. 1(b)).
An OADM is based on a wavelength selective switch fabric and requires wavelength multiplexers and demultiplexers and line power amplifiers. Power to be supplied to the OADM nodes is assumed to be directly proportional to the number of
OADM ports, i.e., to the passing-by lightpaths and locally added/dropped lightpaths. The overall power for the optical layer, i.e., for operating the OADM and
the amplifiers, is therefore considered proportional to the number of OADM ports.

---

[1] Power consumption for compensation of linear and non-linear impairments (e.g., for
  dispersion compensation) can be easily accounted by aggregating its amount to the
  power consumption of the amplifiers or the E/O (O/E) interfaces.

2.3 Powering the Electronic Layer

The electronic layer (e.g., based on IP/MPLS or other technologies) is responsible for processing the data and aggregating the traffic. The process is taking place at the digital cross-connect (DXC) (Fig. 1(c)). Power consumption of a DXC is considered directly proportional to the number of input and output DXC ports, i.e., line terminating equipment and local tributary interfaces.

3   Network Architecture Design

Based on the equipment described above, the problem of designing a WDM ring can be formulated as follows. Given a unidirectional ring topology and the traffic rate of the demands to be supported, the purpose of the design problem is to select the set of lightpaths that are necessary to carry the offered traffic demands. (The routing of the traffic demands is predetermined by the unidirectional ring topology.) The set of lightpaths determine the equipment to be installed (e.g., number of transmitters and receivers, number of DXC and OADM ports) and thus the power that the network will consume.

The optimal design from the CAPEX perspective is the design at minimum equipment installation cost. Typical objective functions for CAPEX-optimal solutions are the minimization of the wavelength cost and/or the minimization of the E/O and O/E interfaces costs [4].

The optimal design from the OPEX perspective (i.e., power consumption) is the design that requires the minimum amount of power to operate the network. The objective function for an OPEX-optimized design can defined according to the power budget model explained in Section 2.

Next, the design problem at minimum CAPEX or at minimum OPEX are discussed for the three considered architectures.

3.1 First Generation (FG) Design

In FG ring networks, nodes are equipped with DXC only. FG ring design consists of lightpaths that are established between physically adjacent nodes. Traffic grooming is performed at each node.

Optimal design at minimum CAPEX can be obtained in polynomial time [4]. The optimal design at minimum CAPEX is also an optimal design at minimum OPEX (i.e., power consumption), for the proposed power budget model.

3.2 Single-Hop (SH) Design

In SH ring networks, nodes are equipped with OADM only. SH ring design consists of tributary signals that are transmitted using a single lightpath, i.e., all-optically from the source to the destination with a single (optical) hop. Traffic grooming between tributary signals that belong to distinct traffic demands, i.e., distinct node pairs, is not possible.

Optimal design at minimum CAPEX can be obtained in polynomial time [4]. The optimal design at minimum CAPEX is also an optimal design at minimum OPEX (i.e., power consumption), for the proposed power budget model.

3.3   Multi-Hop (MH) Design

In MH ring networks, the nodes are equipped with hybrid add-drop multiplexers (HADM), which consists of an OADM and DXC as shown in Fig. 2(a). In the OADM, lightpaths can be transparently transmitted, added or dropped. Traffic of the dropped lightpaths can be aggregated in the DXC, along with the local traffic. Therefore, in a MH network, the traffic is transmitted using a concatenation of lightpaths, thus requiring multiple optical hops. Designing a MH network aims at finding the set of lightpaths and thus the nodes at which the traffic must undergo optical-electrical-optical conversion.

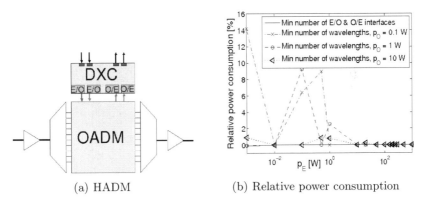

(a) HADM   (b) Relative power consumption

Fig. 2. MH architecture: HADM node (a), relative power consumption [%] vs. p_E for different designs at minimum OPEX among those at minimum CAPEX (b)

Optimal design at minimum CAPEX is NP-hard problem. Heuristic algorithms and linear programming (LP) formulations are available [4]. In [4], MH design is shown to be cost-effective with respect to SH and FG architectures when either the wavelength cost or the interface cost or their joint cost is used as minimization function. This cost-effectiveness is achieved thanks to the possibility to exploit the optical transparency in the OADMs and traffic grooming capabilities in the DXCs.

Optimal design at minimum OPEX is also NP-hard problem. The relation between the CAPEX-optimized design and the OPEX-optimized design is discussed next on a case study.

4   Results

This section presents and compares the power required by the various WDM ring architectures, optimally designed for CAPEX or OPEX minimization. Numerical results are optimally found by a commercially available LP solver, under the following assumptions. The unidirectional ring consists of 6 nodes. Transmission rate of lightpaths is 40 Gb/s. The matrix of traffic demands is complete and uniform. Unless otherwise stated, the rate of traffic demands is 10 Gb/s. Power required for E/O and O/E interfaces of each lightpath is 5 W, as quantified in [2] for commercial products operating at 40 Gb/s.

Let p_E indicate the power consumption of the electrical layer per DXC port. Let p_O indicate the power consumption of the optical layer per OADM port. The network power consumption is thus expressed as function of p_E and p_O and includes also the power required for E/O and O/E interfaces.

As indicated in Section 2, a CAPEX-optimal design of SH ring or a FG ring is also an OPEX-optimal design. Fig. 2(b) quantifies the additional power (in percentage) required in a CAPEX-optimal MH ring with respect to the OPEX-optimal MH ring, for different values of p_E and p_O. Two objective functions for CAPEX minimization are considered: minimization of the maximum number of lightpaths on a link and minimization of the number of E/O and O/E interfaces. Among the CAPEX-optimal solutions, the one at minimum OPEX is then selected. The figure shows that neglecting the OPEX in the planning may lead to an increase of OPEX costs, that in some cases, may be 14 % or even higher. This happens when the objective is the minimization of the maximum number of lightpaths on a link and for low values of p_E and p_O. This finding is also confirmed when the rate of traffic demands varies, as shown in Fig. 3(a) for $p_E = p_O = 200$ mW and for rates between 3 and 40 Gb/s.

Figs. 3(b)-4(b) compare the power consumption of the OPEX-optimal design in FG, SH, and MH rings. Fig. 3(b) quantifies the power consumption versus the rate of each traffic demand, when $p_E = p_O = 200$ mW. For such rates, SH architecture requires always one lightpath for each connection. Thus, power consumption is independent from the load. In FG and MH architectures, power consumption increases with the rate as a large number of lightpaths is required.

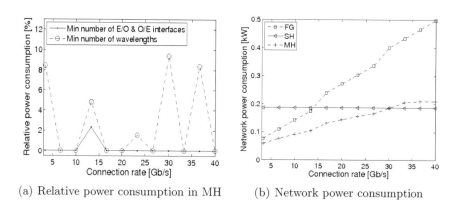

(a) Relative power consumption in MH   (b) Network power consumption

Fig. 3. Power consumption vs. rate: designs at minimum OPEX among those at minimum CAPEX, for MH (a), designs at minimum OPEX for FG, SH, and MH (b)

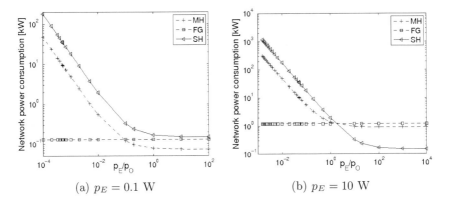

Fig. 4. Network power consumption vs. p_E/p_O for $p_E = 0.1$ W (a) and $p_E = 10$ W (b)

The break-even point between FG and SH indicates that the use of just optics may save power at high load, i.e., when traffic grooming may not help to further reduce the resources utilization and, thus, the drained power.

Figs. 4(a) and 4(b) quantify the power consumption versus the ratio of p_E/p_O, when $p_E = 0.1$ W and 10 W, respectively. When p_O decreases (i.e., the ratio increases), MH may drain less power than FG, because it can exploit the power-efficient optical layer. However, for such values of p_O, if p_E is also high (Fig. 4(b)), SH is more power-efficient than MH. This controversial result is due to the more complex node architecture (i.e., HADM) in MH networks, consisting of both DXC and OADM. This leads to power consumption for both the electronic and the optical layer components, yielding a higher overall power consumption.

5   Conclusion

The paper discussed the problem of accounting the OPEX, due to equipment power consumption, during the design of optical networks with traffic grooming capabilities. A power budget model that accounts for power dissipation at the optical layer, electrical layer, and E/O and O/E interfaces was proposed and applied to the design of a unidirectional WDM ring with first-generation, single-hop, or multi-hop architecture.

While, in general, the design at minimal CAPEX is also at minimal OPEX in SH and FG networks, this may not hold anymore in MH networks. It was found that an OPEX-oblivious design may require up to more than 14% additional power.

When optimizing the OPEX, the most power-efficient architecture depends on the power consumption of the different layers and their interfaces. Interestingly, MH architecture that is known to be most CAPEX-efficient [4] may not be the most OPEX-efficient. MH is more flexible and can exploit optical transparency and traffic grooming capabilities at the nodes. But, the increased flexibility may require a more complex node architecture that, in turn, drains more power.

These results permit to derive also insightful guidelines for reducing the power consumption in optical networks, e.g., utilization of node architectures that are more power-efficient and can provide optical transparency and traffic grooming capabilities, introduction of innovative node architectures that, for instance, can selectively switch-off components (i.e., the DXC or the OADM in an HADM), study of innovative network designs that exploit the power-efficient equipment.

References

1. An inefficient truth. Technical report, Global Action Plan (2007)
2. Butler, K.: Predictive models for power dissipation in optical transceivers. Master's thesis, Massachusetts Institute of Technology (2004)
3. Cardona Restrepo, J.C., Gruber, C., Mas Machuca, C.: Energy profile aware routing. In: ICC conf. proc. (2009)
4. Cerutti, I., Fumagalli, A., Tacca, M., Lardies, A., Jagannathan, R.: The Multi-Hop Multi-Rate Wavelength Division Multiplexing ring. JLT 18(12) (2000)
5. Cerutti, I., Valcarenghi, L., Castoldi, P.: Power saving architectures for unidirectional wdm rings. In: OFC proc. (2009)
6. Ceuppens, L., Sardella, A., Kharitonov, D.: Power saving strategies and technologies in network equipment opportunities and challenges, risk and rewards. In: Proc. Int. Symposium on Applications and the Internet (2008)
7. Chabarek, J., Sommers, J., Barford, P., Estan, C., Tsiang, D., Wright, S.: Power awareness in network design and routing. In: Proc. IEEE INFOCOM (2008)
8. Chiaraviglio, L., Mellia, M., Neri, F.: Energy-aware networks: reducing power consumption by switching off network elements. In: Proc. FEDERICA-Phosporus tutorial and workshop (2008)
9. Metz, B., Davidson, O., Bosch, P., Dave, R., Meyer, L.: Mitigation of climate change. Technical report, Intergovernmental Panel on Climate Change (IPCC) Working Group III Report (2007), http://www.ipcc.ch
10. Pickavet, M., Demeester Puype, P., Colle, D.: Power reduction techniques in multilayer traffic engineering. In: ICTON conf. proc. (2009)
11. The Climate Group. SMART 2020: Enabling the low carbon economy in the information age. Technical report, Global eSustainability Initiative, GeSI (2008)
12. Tucker, R.S.: The role of optics and electronics in high-capacity routers. IEEE/OSA Journal of Lightwave Technology 24(12), 4655–4673 (2006)
13. Tucker, R.S.: Optical packet switched WDM networks: a cost and energy perspective. In: Proc. Optical Fiber Communication Conference (2008)

Energy Efficiency in Thin Client Solutions

Willem Vereecken, Lien Deboosere, Pieter Simoens, Brecht Vermeulen,
Didier Colle, Chris Develder, Mario Pickavet, Bart Dhoedt, and Piet Demeester

Ghent University - IBBT, Department of Information Technology (INTEC)
Gaston Crommenlaan 8, Bus 201, 9050 Ghent, Belgium
`firstname.lastname@intec.ugent.be`

Abstract. In current society it is becoming more and more important
to take energy efficiency considerations into account when designing information and communication technology (ICT) solutions. In ICT, vir-
tualisation is being regarded as a way to increase energy efficiency. One
such virtualization solution which can be realized trough grids or cloud
computing is the thin client paradigm. This paper analyses the energy
saving opportunities of the thin client paradigm.

1 Introduction

The current image of ICT is rather environmentally friendly. The worldwide
communication via datacom and telecom networks has transformed society and
created opportunities to reduce global energy consumption and CO_2 emissions
in general. However, the ubiquitousness of ICT in daily life has caused its share
in the global energy consumption to increase drastically. It is to be expected
that this share will grow even more in the coming years. ICT related energy
consumption can be estimated at 4% of the primary energy production in 2008.
Forecasts for 2020 are typically in the range of 8% [1].

Currently the power saving solutions for ICT were based on the principle
of downscaling the performance of devices and even shutting them down when
possible. A good example is mobile computing where devices need to be power
efficient in order to maximize battery lifetime. On the other hand, power can be
saved by assuring that a certain task is performed on the location where it will
consume the least ammount of energy.

The power saving potential of this solution can be analysed with the thin
client paradigm [2]. This approach is similar to the mainframe approach generally
adopted in the '60s-'70s (and left again in the early '80s), where a server farm
is performing the computational intensive (and hence energy hungry) functions,
while the rendering for the end-user is done on very constrained devices.

Thin client solutions are currently implemented mainly driven by the objective
to reduce equipment cost and increase manageability. In this paper, however, we
will analyse the implications of the thin client paradigm on power consumption
at the customer premise, in the network and in the data center. Based on this
analysis we will try to determine the key aspects to consider when designing a
power efficient thin client solution.

T. Doulamis et al.: (Eds.): GridNets 2009, LNICST 25, pp. 109–116, 2010.

2 Mathemathical Model

In order to determine the energy efficiency we will compare the power consumption of a standalone desktop with the power consumption of a thin client solution. For the thin client solution we consider the power consumption at the user premises, in the access network and in the data center. These cases are schematically depicted in Fig. 1.

Note that we are fully allocating the power consumption in the network to the thin client solution. This is first to set clear boundaries for the analysis. Secondly, the thin client paradigm will be responsible for the majority of the traffic between the client terminal and the server ($0Mb/s - 5Mb/s$[3]).

2.1 Desktop, Client Terminal and Server

We will consider a linear model for the power consumption of a desktop computer (d), a thin client terminal (c) and a server (s). This power consumption will depend on the CPU load for running the application, denoted as λ^*_{CPU}, a number between 0 and 100%. The influence of the network traffic on the power consumption is negligable for the considered bandwidth. Thus, the model for a computer is (* = d,c,s):

$$P^* = P^*_0 + \alpha^*_{CPU}\lambda^*_{CPU} \tag{1}$$

For the client terminal, the power consumption appears to be constant even with varying CPU load λ^c_{CPU}.

On the server, we need to determine the dependency between λ^s_{CPU} and λ^d_{CPU}. Every calculation that needs to be performed on the desktop computer, needs to be performed on the server. Moreover, on the server there is also an overhead of the thin client protocol.

In order to be able to compare the CPU's on both the desktop and the server we denote the processing capacity of a server (according to a relevant performance oriented benchmark such as SPEC CINT2006 [4]) as C^s and the analogous parameter for the desktop case C^d. Since SPEC CINT2006 is a single threaded benchmark, we define the processing capacity as:

$$C^* = \#cores \times CINT2006 \tag{2}$$

We denote ϵ as the extra load per user caused by the thin client protocol. When we assume a share ratio of N users per server, the the CPU load on the server is:

$$\lambda^s_{CPU} = N\left[\lambda^d_{CPU}\frac{C^d}{C^s} + \epsilon\right] \tag{3}$$

In [5], [6], [7] and [8] we can find data on the power consumption of desktops, laptops, servers and thin client devices respectively. In [4] we find reports with the CINT2006 benchmark.

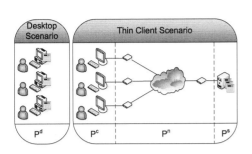

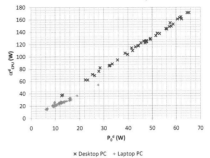

Fig. 1. Desktop and Thin Client Scenario

Fig. 2. Power consumption of Desktop and Laptop PC's

2.2   The Network

In order to limit the network latency we assume the data center to be located in the access network. In [9] target values for the power consumption of the network equipment are given.

2.3   Cooling

The servers are located in a data center. In a data center we also need to account for power consumption of HVAC, UPS, etc. This factor is denoted by the Power Usage Effectiveness (PUE) [10], the total power consumption of the data center, divided by the power consumption of the ICT equipment. Since our model should cover multiple cases we will consider the PUE accounted for in the relevant parameters.

2.4   Total Power Consumption of the Thin Client Solution

In summary, the power consumption for one user in the thin client paradigm is:

$$P^{tc} = P_0^c + P^n + \frac{P_0^s}{N} + \alpha_{CPU}^s \left[\lambda_{CPU}^d \frac{C^d}{C^s} + \epsilon \right] \tag{4}$$

3   Equipment Selection

3.1   Desktop PC

In Fig. 2 we have the values for P_0^d and α_{CPU}^d for the category A, B and C computers from [5] and [6]. We see there is a strong correlation between P_0^d and α_{CPU}^d. For a desktop PC we can roughly say $\frac{\alpha_{CPU}^d}{P_0^d} = 2.66$ and $\frac{\alpha_{CPU}^d}{P_0^d} = 2.12$ for a laptop PC.

The power consumption of a laptop is also significantly lower than the power consumption of a desktop. However, this is not a fair comparison. The laptop PC performs exactly the same functionality as the desktop PC while only consuming a fraction of the power. This is because the laptop PC is optimized for maximal battery lifetime. This is not the case for all other devices used in the thin client solution. Therefore we want to compare technologies which are on the same level of power efficiency while clearly indicating that power optimizations of the involved equipment and an improved PUE in the data center will be required for the thin client paradigm to become a power efficient technology.

Based on these results we have selected the desktop *Dell OptiPlex360 (Intel Core 2 Duo E7400)* as a reference desktop computer. Its power consumption and processing capacity are summerized in table 1(a).

The average load λ_{CPU}^d will be approximately 10% on the desktop PC which is largely sufficient for standard office applications such as text editors and spreadsheets.

3.2   Thin Client Terminal

In [8] an overview is given of power consumption data for client terminals. This data is presented in Fig. 3.

For most devices the power consumption is comparable to that of a laptop PC. This is due to the amount of processing capacity and other functionality on the device. In some cases one cannot speak of a 'thin' client anymore and the term 'lean' client is used. In this study we want the capacity of the client device to be limited to only input-output signals. Therefore we use a representative *Wyse S10* device.

3.3   Server

For the servers there is less correlation between P_0^s and α_{CPU}^s. Moreover, we will try to have a maximal number of users on each server. This means $\lambda_{CPU}^s \approx 1$.

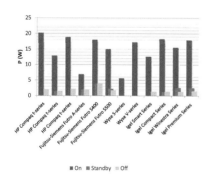

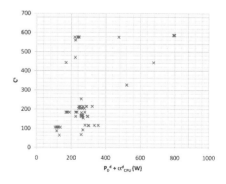

Fig. 3. Power Consumption of Client Terminals

Fig. 4. Processing Capacity of Servers in function of their Maximal Power Consumption

Table 1. Equipment Parameters

(a) Computers

Desktop PC	P_0^d	39.764W
	α_{CPU}^d	103.736W
	C^d	2×23
Client Terminal	P_0^c	5.6W
Server	P_0^s	65W
	α_{CPU}^s	155W
	C^s	16×36
	PUE	2

(b) Network Equipment (per user)

	User Prem. Eq.	Access Netw. Eq.	Total
	Active state		
ADSL2	3.8 W	1.2 W	5.0 W
VDSL2	6.0 W	1.8 W	7.8 W
PON	7.7 W	11.0 W/32	8.04 W
	Reduced Power State		
ADSL2	2.6 W	0.4 W	3.0 W
VDSL2	3.5 W	0.6 W	4.1 W
PON	4.0 W	0.0 W	4.0 W

When we want to have an energy efficient solution we want the processing capacity per consumed power to be as high as possible. In Fig. 4 both values are given. In [7] we find with power consumption data and [4] provides us with the CINT2006 benchmark.

Generally speaking the power consumption scales with growing capacity. This is logical since C^s scales with the number of cores. There are however some servers which demonstrate a high capacity compared to the power consumption. Therefore we select a *ASUSTeK Computer ASUS RS160-E5 (2 × Intel Xeon L5420 Processor, 2.50 GHz)*. Its power consumption and processing capacity are summerized in table 1(a). The server overhead ϵ of the thin client protocol is considered to be small ($\epsilon \approx 0$). We also assume the server to be located in a data center with a typical PUE of 2 [11].

3.4   Network

Finally, for the network power consumption we will base the used values on the target values mentioned in [9]. We consider three network technologies: ADSL2, VDSL2 and PON. The network power consumption values are summarized in table 1(b).

4   Quantification

4.1   Active State Analysis

Fig. 5 displays a breakdown in the power consumption for a desktop PC and a thin client setup. We have assumed the maximal share ratio of N=125 on the servers.

Compared to the desktop PC, the power consumption of Thin Client Setup is significantly lower. We also notice that the power consumption of the thin client solution does not contain a dominant factor. This means that power optimizations at user premises, in the network and in the data center are equally important. For example, one would expect the PON solution to be most power

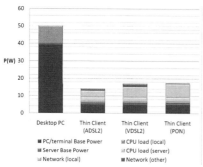

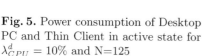

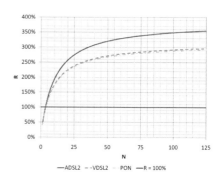

Fig. 5. Power consumption of Desktop PC and Thin Client in active state for $\lambda_{CPU}^d = 10\%$ and N=125

Fig. 6. Power Saving Ratio (R) in function of the Server Share Ratio (N)

efficient, but due to the high power consumption of the local gateway at the user premises, this advantage is lost.

We evaluate the power saving ratio $R = \frac{P^d}{P^{tc}}$ which expresses the relative power saving between both scenarios. The criterium for power efficiency is $R > 100\%$

In Fig. 6 R is displayed in function of the server share ratio N. We see the thin client solution is already very power efficient with low share ratio's. On the other hand we see that, depending on the network technology, power saving ratio's up to 350% are achievable.

4.2   Passive State Analysis

In the previous section we have assumed that all users are active. This is however not always the case. In this section we investigate the influence of passive users. We denote the number of active users as N_{act}^u and the number of passive users as N_{off}^u. Obviously, we always have:

$$N^u = N_{act}^u + N_{off}^u \tag{5}$$

For the desktop, client terminal and server we will assume that the device is either active or switched off. When a device is switched off it means it can be physically cut off from its power supply. In reality, this is not always the case and often there is a (low) standby power consumption. However, since we are aiming for a power efficient solution we will assume we cut off the power when a device is switched off.

In the network we do not cut off the devices since we want to keep a minimal connectivity between the user premise and the data center in order to be able to send wake-up signals to the devices. The reduced power state power consumption is given in table 1(b).

In Fig. 7 we have displayed R in function of the passive user fraction. The desktop power consumption P^d scales with the number of active users since all

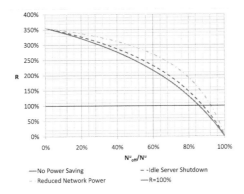

Fig. 7. Power Saving Ratio of ADSL2 case in function of the fraction of passive users with $\lambda_{CPU}^d = 10\%$ and $N = 125$

equipment is switched off for a passive user. For the thin client scenario we have three different cases.

No Power Saving. When we do not mitigate for the passive users and all the servers remain active the efficiency degrades approximately linearly in function of the fraction of passive users $\frac{N_{off}^u}{N^u}$. This can be explained because $P^t c_{PC}$ almost remains constant while P^d reduces linearly. The only factor reducing the power consumption of the thin client scenario is the switched off client terminal.

Idle Server Shutdown. We can however measure the number of active users and only switch on the required number of servers so that the active servers are used at their full capacity and the passive servers are switched off.

Reduced Network Power. On top of that we can also use a reduced power state to connect the passive users to the data center which leads to an even more optimized power consumption.

It is clear that the optimization solutions allow for an increasing number of passive users to keep the thin client solution more efficient than the desktop solution. In this case a passive user fraction of 93% is achievable.

5   Conclusions

In this paper we created an analytical model in order to investigate the power efficiency of the thin client paradigm.

Comparing the paradigm with a laptop PC has shown that power optimizations of the individual equipment and the datacentre PUE will be required. However, when comparing with technology with a similar level of energy optimization (desktop PC) the thin client paradigm shows a clear potential.

The case study displayed that power savings up to 350% are possible. However, this potential is impaired by a reduced efficiency when a fraction of the users is passive. This can be mitigated by selectively switching off servers when reduced activity occurs. Secondly, introducing reduced power states in the network make the thin client paradigm more power efficient for idle user ratio's up to 93%.

Acknowledgements. The work described in this paper was carried out with the support of the BONE project ("Building the Future Optical Network in Europe"), a Network of Excellence funded by the European Community's Seventh Framework. Part of the research leading to these results was done for the MobiThin Project and has received funding from the European Community's Seventh Framework (FP7/2007-2013) under grant agreement nr 216946. C. Develder is supported by a grant from the Research Foundation - Flanders (FWO) as a post-doctoral researcher.

References

1. Pickavet, M., Vereecken, W., Demeyer, S., Audenaert, P., Vermeulen, B., Develder, C., Colle, D., Dhoedt, B., Demeester, P.: Worldwide energy needs for ICT: the rise of power-aware networking. In: IEEE ANTS 2008 (December 2008)
2. Knermann, C., Hiebel, M., Paum, H., Rettweiler, M., Schroder, A.: Environmental comparison of the relevance of pc and thin client desktop equipment for the climate. Fraunhofer UMSICHT (2008)
3. Deboosere, L., De Wachter, J., De Turck, F., Dhoedt, B., Demeester, P.: Thin Client Computing Solutions in Low- and High-Motion Scenarios. In: International Conference on Networking and Services (ICNS), p. 38 (2007)
4. Standard Performance Evaluation Corporation, Spec cpu2006, (July 2009), http://www.spec.org/cpu2006/
5. Energy Star, Qualified desktops and integrated computers, (July 2009), http://www.energystar.gov
6. Energy Star, Qualified notebooks and tablet computers (July 2009), http://www.energystar.gov
7. Standard Performance Evaluation Corporation, Specpower ssj2008 results (July 2009), http://www.spec.org/powerssj2008/results/
8. The Danish Electricity Saving Trust, See the trust's data covering power used by different thin clients (March 2009), http://www.savingtrust.dk/
9. European Commission, Code of conduct on energy consumption of broadband equipment version 3 (November 2008)
10. The Green Grid, Green grid metrics: Describing datacenter power efficiency (February 2007), http://www.thegreengrid.org
11. Scheihing, P.: Creating energy-efficient data centers. In: Data Center Facilities and Engineering Conference (May 2007)

Wireless Grids Workshop

Architecture to Integrate Broadband Access Networks and Wireless Grids

João Paulo Ribeiro Pereira

Instituto Politécnico de Bragança (IPB)
Bragança, Portugal
jprp@ipb.pt

Abstract. Today, the access networks face two main challenges: the increasing bandwidth demand and mobility trends. All this will require fundamental changes to the operations of access networks, the functionality of network nodes and the architecture itself. By other side, the evolution of computing and communication networks toward decentralized and distributed systems implies that all the intelligence is on the edge nodes of the networks. Integrating wireless devices with the traditional wired grid infrastructure will allow the access (transfer, processing, etc) to the information that is now scattered across the different devices. In this paper, we present a new architecture and a cost model to support the new requirements of broadband access (fixed and nomadic users) and wireless grids in an integrated way

Keywords: Wireless Grids, Access Networks, Broadband Access Technologies, Techno-economic Cost Model.

1 Introduction

Actually, the development of wireless technology and mobile devices enable us to access the network services from anywhere at any time [1]. The wireless devices (mobile phones, PDAs, laptops, sensors, etc) have an important role in our daily. Computing and communication networks have evolved from centralized, hierarchical systems under the management of a single entity toward decentralized, distributed systems under the collective management of many entities. Today, all the intelligence is in the edge nodes of the networks, which implies that information is now scattered across the different devices [2] [3].

By other side, the increasing demand of "quad-play" (also known as quadruple-play) services, including video, voice, data and mobility, have created new challenges to the modern broadband wireless/wired access networks [4]. Actually, the access networks face two main challenges: the increasing bandwidth demand and mobility trends. All this will require fundamental changes to the operations of access networks, the functionality of network nodes, and the architecture itself.

In this context, we propose a techno-economic model to support the new requirements of broadband access (fixed and nomadic users) and wireless grids in an integrated way (Figure 1). The approach has two main objectives: a) Provide broadband access to end users, and b) Support the implementation of wireless grids (our

T. Doulamis et al.: (Eds.): GridNets 2009, LNICST 25, pp. 119–130, 2010.

architecture assumes that the wireless grids must have some access to the access network infrastructure).The final result is an integrated architecture that includes the 2 main components: Broadband access and wireless grids.

2 Framework

2.1 Broadband Access Networks

The requirements for bandwidth capacity have increased significantly over the last several years [5]. The requirements for services such as HDTV, video conferences, peer-to-peer traffic, etc., have led to predictions of bandwidth consumption of at least 50Mbps downstream for residential consumers and in the region of 8 Mbps upstream [6]. The "triple play" services (Internet, telephone and TV services), lead to a great increase in bandwidth demand. However, the existing access networks are not able to support this increase and the capacity to deliver broadband services remains a challenge ("last mile problem"). The access network remains a bottleneck in terms of the bandwidth and service quality it affords the end user.

Besides the bandwidth, other great challenge to access networks is the mobility and the user needs to have internet access anywhere and anytime. The mobility of the end-user will also introduce an unprecedented volatility to the network architecture [7;8]. Nomadicity causes end-users to pop up and disappear at different locations in the network.

2.2 Wireless Grids

Wireless Grid (WG) is an emerging communication and resource sharing architecture that has been discussed in recent years. The WG expand the scope of resources to include peripherals: display, camera, microphone, etc. Wireless peripherals and the access device form an ad hoc network and communicate with each other and allow the ad hoc sharing of resources (e.g., microphones, screens, processing power) of edge devices (e.g., mobile phone, laptop, PDA) [9]. In a wireless grid, the edge nodes are the network.

A large number of these devices arrive and depart frequently on wireless grids. Then, as wireless devices have different spatial behavior, they are divided into 3 main categories: Mobile, nomadic and fixed-location wireless devices. Wireless grid solutions offer to home broadband users, the maximum ability to share necessary documents, DVDs, music, displays, cameras, printers, sensors and so on [10].

2.3 Cost Model Framework

The proposed model considers two main parts (see figure 1): Broadband Access and Wireless Grids. Broadband access part analyses two perspectives: static layer and nomadic layer. The proposed model considers that in the static layer, users are stationary and normally require data, voice, and video quality services (these subscribers demand great bandwidth). In the nomadic layer (or mobility layer), the main concern is mobility and normally the required bandwidth is smaller than in the static layer. The focus of the wireless networks was to support mobility and flexibility, while for the wired access networks is bandwidth and high QoS [4]. To support the static layer we consider five technologies: FTTH(PON), DSL, HFC, PLC, and WiMAX. For the nomadic layer we chose the WiMAX solution.

To support the Wireless Grids part we consider several technologies: Wi-Fi, Bluetooth, UWB, ZigBee, 3G, etc. As we can see in figure 1, our model divides the area into several access networks, and we can have different solutions for each one.

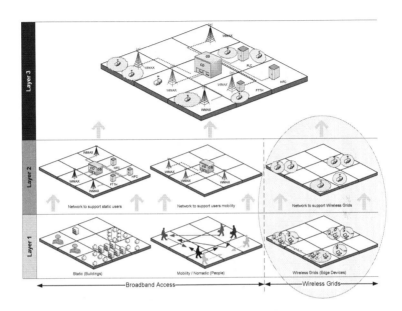

Fig. 1. Cost model framework

Methodology used for Broadband Access: As we can see in Figure 1, the framework is divided into three main layers:

- (Layer 1) First, we identify for each sub-area the total households and SMEs (Static analysis), and total nomadic users (Mobility analysis). The proposed model initially separates these two components because they have different characteristics.
- (Layer 2) In this layer, the best solution for each access network is analyzed (static and nomadic perspective). For the static analysis we consider Fiber to the Home (FTTH- PON), Digital Subscriber Line (DSL), Hybrid Fiber Coax (HFC), Power Line Communications (PLC) and WiMAX technologies, and for the nomadic analysis we use the WiMAX technology. Then, the final result of this layer is the best technological solution to support the different needs (Static and nomadic). The selection of the best option is based in four output results: NPV, IRR, Cost per subscriber in year 1, and Cost per subscriber in year n.
- (Layer 3) The next step is the construction of a single infrastructure that supports the two components. To this end, the tool analyses for each access network which is the best solution (based on NPV, IRR, etc). Finally, for each

sub-area we verify if the best solution is: a) The wired technologies (FTTH, DSL, HFC, and PLC) to support the static component and the WiMAX technology for mobility; or b) The use of WiMAX technology to support the fixed and nomadic component.

Methodology used for Wireless Grids: (Layer 1) First, we identify for each sub-area the total HH (residential) and SMEs (school, hospital, etc.) with wireless grids. (Layer 2) In this layer , the model identifies the necessary components to support the wireless grids. Finally, in layer 3 we propose an integrated architecture.

4   Cost Model

The model focuses the access part of the network (that starts at CO and end at the subscriber CPE) and the wireless grids.

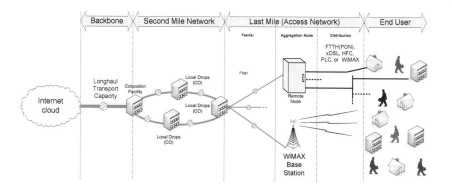

Fig. 2. General System Architecture

4.1   Access Network Architecture

To provide BB access, our model considers five technologies: FTTH(PON), HFC, xDSL, PLC, and WiMAX. The outside segment is divided into three main parts (see Figure 3) [5]: Feeder, Aggregation Nodes and Distribution (for HFC technology the distribution segment is divided into distribution and drop).

Feeder segment is the network between the CO and the aggregation nodes. The model includes not only the cost of equipment (Fiber repeaters), but also the optical fiber cables, installation, trenches, and housing (street cabinets) costs. The ducts can be shared by several optical fiber cables.

The aggregation nodes are located in access areas street cabinets. The components of these nodes depend on the technology. In the next paragraphs we will present the elements for the five technologies in study.

The distribution network links the aggregation nodes with CPE. Like feeder networks, in distribution, the model includes not only the cost of equipment (copper, coax, and LV grid repeaters), but also the cables, installation and trenches costs.

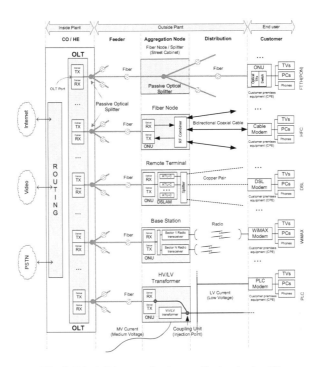

Fig. 3. Block Diagram for Access Technologies [4]

4.2 Wireless Grid Architecture

Wireless grid architecture is mainly consisted of backbone networks and wireless ad hoc sub networks, partially similar to P2P network [11]. To [3], wireless grids are limited by the device resources, and there is a typical architecture that a backbone grid comprised of wired and fixed grid devices, several access grid comprised of wireless devices which can access the processing, storage, bandwidth of backbone grid. Access grid connects to backbone grid by wireless mode, such as Ultra Wideband (UWB), ZigBee, WLAN, Cellular network (2G/2.5G/3G/B3G/4G), etc (see table 1).

Table 1. Wireless Technologies (WLAN and WPAN)

	Wi-Fi	UWB	Bluetooth	ZigBee	3.5G
Standard	802.11g	802.15.3a	802.15.1	802.15.4	UTRA FDD R5
Usage	WLAN	WPAN	WPAN	WPAN	3.5 G
Throughput	54Mbps (20 m) 6 Mbps (60 m)	55-480 Mbps	2-3 Mbps	250 Kbps	1.8 to 14.4Mbps
Range	100m	< 10m	10 m	50 m	5000 m
Frequency	2.4 GHz	3.1 – 10.6 GHz	2.4 GHz	2.4 GHz	Tx: 1920-1980 MHz Rx: 2110-2170MHz

In the proposed architecture (see Figure 4), edge devices are connected via ad-hoc wireless networks, and the devices may come and go (i.e. spatial behavior). The architecture assumes that the wireless grids must have some access to the access network infrastructure. The architecture uses an edge interface (Edge router) to connect the wireless grids to the broadband infrastructure (Access Network). Then, the wireless grid solutions offer to broadband users the maximum ability to share documents, music, cameras, displays, printers, sensors and so on.

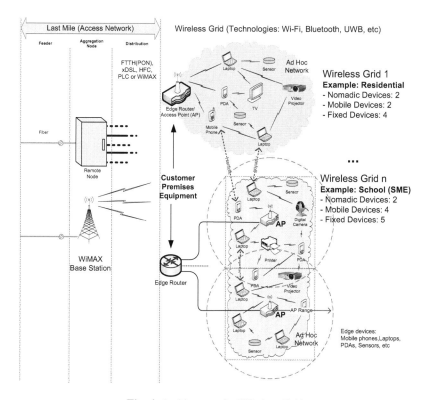

Fig. 4. Architecture for Wireless Grids

As referred above, in our model we consider that the edge devices are divided into 3 types: Nomadic, mobile and fixed. The wireless grid connects to backbone by wireless mode (Wi-Fi technology). The wireless links between the edge devices in the wireless grids can be supported by several wireless technologies (see Table 1): Wi-Fi, Bluetooth, UWB, ZigBee, 3G, etc. Then, in each wireless grid, the devices can use the Wi-Fi links (in our model, the Wi-Fi signal is propagated in all area of the wireless grid), or other technology (Bluetooth, UWB, etc) if the device don't has the Wi-Fi technology.

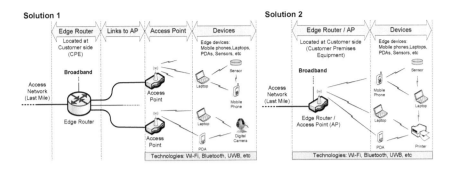

Fig. 5. Block diagram of Wireless Grids systems architecture

As we can see in figure 5, our model divides the wireless grid system architecture into two or four main segments (depend on the solution): edge router, link to access point equipment, access point equipment, and devices. The components used to compute the results for wireless grids are presented in the next table. The costs of devices are supported by the costumers.

Table 2. Wireless Grids architecture components

Edge Router	Links to APs	Wireless Access Points	Devices
1) Router equipment;	1) Cable;	1) AP equipment;	Cost supported by the customer.
2) Equipment installation.	2) Cable installation	2) Equipment installation	1) Equipment: Nomadic, Mobile, and Fixed devices

Geometric Model Assumptions. The geometrical model definition is required to calculate the length of cables (from edge router to wireless gateways) and the total cells required to cover all the wireless grid area (see figure 6).

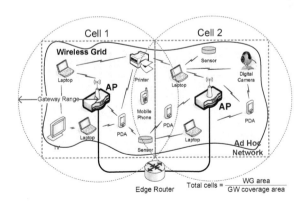

Fig. 6. Geometric model for Wireless Grids

5 Results

5.1 Scenario Description

5.1.1 Scenario Description for Access Network

The three main activities for scenario description are: area definition, definition of the set of services to be offered, and the pricing (see Table 3). Table 3 shows the general input parameters used in our model and tool. The trends for each parameter are presented in the last column. This scenario is defined for a study period of 15 years and for an urban area. The definition of the area type is essential because several costs between urban and rural areas are different.

Table 3. General Input Parameters for Access Network

		Scenario	
		Value	Trend (% per year)
Years (Study Period)		15	
Geographical Area Description		Urban	
Total Access Networks (sub-areas)		4	
Area Characteristics	Area Size (Km2)	45	0,00%
	Access Network area (Km2)	11,25	
	Residential		
	Total Households (potential subscribers)	7600	2,00%
	Households Density (Households / Km2)	169	
	Population Density (people/Km2)	1200	3,80%
	Population	54.000	
	Inhabitants per household	7,11	
	Technology penetration rate (expected market penetration)	50,00%	8,00%
	Number of subscribers	3.800	
	Average Households per building	14	
	Number of buildings in serving area (homes/km2)	543	
	SME (small-to-medium sized enterprises)		
	Total SME in Area	1200	1,50%
	Technology penetration rate (expected market penetration)	40,00%	5,00%
	Total SME (customers)	480	
	Nomadic Users		
	Total Nomadic Users	1500	15,00%
Service Characteristics	**Residential**		
	Required Downstream bandwidth (Mbps): Avg data rate	8	1,2%
	Required Upstream bandwidth (Mbps): Avg data rate	0,512	1,2%
	SME		
	Required Downstream bandwidth (Mbps): Avg data rate	12	1,2%
	Required Upstream bandwidth (Mbps): Avg data rate	0,512	1,2%
	Nomadic Users		
	Required Downstream bandwidth (Mbps): Avg data rate	2	2,0%
	Required Upstream bandwidth (Mbps): Avg data rate	0,512	2,0%
Pricing	**Residential**		
	One-time Activation/connection fee (€)	100	0,15%
	Subscription fee (€ / month)	50	0,15%
	SME		
	One-time Activation/connection fee (€)	150	0,15%
	Subscription fee (€ / month)	75	0,15%
	Nomadic Users		
	One-time Activation/connection fee (€)	75	0,15%
	Subscription fee (€ / month)	45	0,15%
Discount Rate (on cash flows)		0%	

After the general specification, is obligatory the definition of the number of access networks in which we want to divide the area in study is compulsory (between 1 and 36). This scenario assumes the division into 4 sub-areas (or access networks). Following, the definition of the number of households (HH), SMEs and nomadic users is also required, for each access network (see Table 4).

Table 4. Input Parameters for each Access Network

	Access Network 1	Access Network 2	Access Network 3	Access Network 4	Total Area (Year1)
Total HH:	6000	0	500	1100	**7600**
Total SME:	1000	0	150	50	**1200**
Total Nomadic Users:	500	0	1000	0	**1500**

5.1.2 Scenario Description for Wireless Grids

The chosen scenario consists of 2770 residential wireless grids and 555 SMEs with wireless grids (Year 1), uniformly distributed in square area of 45 km2 (table 5). Each mobile and nomadic device selects a random destination within the area (in a specific wireless grid, for mobile devices, and between wireless grids for nomadic devices).

Table 5. Wireless Grids Parameters definition

		Trend (% per year)	Access Network 1	Access Network 2	Access Network 3	Access Network 4	Total Area (Year 1)
	Total HH (Year 1):		6000	0	500	1100	7600
	Total SMEs (Year 1):		1000	0	150	50	1200
Total Grids	**WG distribution**						
	% HH with WG (Residential)	1,50%	40,00%	0,00%	30,00%	20,00%	
	Total HH with WG (Year 1)		2400	0	150	220	2770
	% SME with WG (School, Hospital, etc)	2,00%	45,00%	0,00%	50,00%	60,00%	
	Total SME with WG (Year 1)		450	0	75	30	555
Devices Characteristics	**Devices per WG: HH (Residential)**						
	AVG number of Mobile devices per WG	0,25%	4	0	2	5	11
	AVG number of Nomadic devices per WG	0,50%	2	0	1	3	6
	AVG number of Fixed devices per WG	0,15%	3	0	2	2	7
	Total		9	0	5	10	24
	Devices per WG: SMEs (School, Hospital, Market, etc)						
	AVG number of Mobile devices per WG	0,55%	10	0	5	8	23
	AVG number of Nomadic devices per WG	0,15%	15	0	4	25	44
	AVG number of Fixed devices per WG	0,25%	2	0	5	1	8
	Total		27	0	14	34	75
Area Charact.	**Area per WG: HH**						
	AVG Area of each WG (m2)	0,15%	200	0	175	220	
	Area per WG: SMEs						
	AVG Area of each WG (m2)	0,50%	6000	0	900	1000	

The area is divided into four access networks and each of them has different characteristics. The model divides the wireless grids into two main categories: residential (households) and institutional (schools, hospitals, enterprises, etc.). As said above, we consider that the edge devices are divided into 3 types: Nomadic, mobile and fixed.

Next table shows the technology parameters required to our model: maximum range of gateway equipment, and the cable type used to link the edge router and GW equipment.

Table 6. Wireless Grids Technology Parameters

Max. Range of each Gateway (m)	50,00
Cell width (m2)	5000,00
Cable type	CoaxCable5

The choice of cable is also required to compute the final costs (the data base has several types of cable with the respective cost.

5.2   Results

This section presents the final results to support the new requirements of broadband access (fixed and nomadic users) and Wireless grids. Then, we separate the results into these two parts.

Table 7. Broadband Access General Results

		Access Network 1	Access Network 2	Access Network 3	Access Network 4
	# Fixed Users	7000	0	650	1150
	# Nomadic Users	500	0	1000	0
FTTH	Payback Period	12	0	15	26
	NPV	18.545.019 €	- €	35.266 €	- 3.270.304 €
	IRR	6,11%	0,00%	0,10%	-4,46%
	Cost Subc Y1	8.812 €	- €	12.997 €	16.620 €
	Cost Subc Y15	176 €	- €	221 €	256 €
	CAPEX	42.056.667 €	- €	5.494.978 €	13.136.344 €
	OPEX	8.270.447 €	- €	809.851 €	1.559.015 €
WIMAX	Payback Period	14	0	15	15
	NPV	2.267.422 €	- €	131.193 €	136.279 €
	IRR	1,57%	0,00%	0,91%	0,57%
	Cost Subc Y1	5.050 €	- €	5.584 €	5.094 €
	Cost Subc Y15	482 €	- €	490 €	471 €
	CAPEX	51.478.055 €	- €	4.809.506 €	8.763.517 €
	OPEX	15.126.656 €	- €	1.399.396 €	2.525.258 €
DSL	Payback Period	15	0	28	51
	NPV	690.024 €	- €	- 2.373.143 €	- 9.427.161 €
	IRR	0,18%	0,00%	-5,52%	-10,60%
	Cost Subc Y1	12.860 €	- €	18.761 €	24.487 €
	Cost Subc Y15	203 €	- €	262 €	329 €
	CAPEX	59.457.479 €	- €	7.839.295 €	19.126.195 €
	OPEX	8.724.630 €	- €	873.944 €	1.726.021 €
HFC	Payback Period	13	0	20	30
	NPV	13.058.160 €	- €	- 551.645 €	- 4.612.118 €
	IRR	3,91%	0,00%	-1,47%	-5,90%
	Cost Subc Y1	10.181 €	- €	14.552 €	18.506 €
	Cost Subc Y15	179 €	- €	218 €	266 €
	CAPEX	47.412.355 €	- €	6.063.773 €	14.424.870 €
	OPEX	8.401.617 €	- €	827.968 €	1.612.302 €
PLC	Payback Period	19	0	28	42
	NPV	- 5.695.712 €	- €	- 2.430.750 €	- 8.305.119 €
	IRR	-1,40%	0,00%	-5,49%	-9,11%
	Cost Subc Y1	14.187 €	- €	19.252 €	23.872 €
	Cost Subc Y15	223 €	- €	257 €	291 €
	CAPEX	64.182.225 €	- €	7.723.562 €	17.656.236 €
	OPEX	10.385.620 €	- €	1.047.284 €	2.073.937 €

Table 7 shows the results for the use of the several technologies to support the static layer (HH and SMEs). Each column corresponds to an access network. The output variables are represented in the lines: Payback period, NPV, IRR, Cost per subscriber in year 1, and cost per subscriber in year n.

Table 8. Wireless Grids General Results

Total Years: 15		Access Network 1	Access Network 2	Access Network 3	Access Network 4	Total Area
Wireless Grids distribution						
Year 1	Total Residential Wireless Grids	2400	0	150	220	2770
	Total Institutional Wireless Grids	450	0	75	30	555
	Total WG (Residential + SME)	2850	0	225	250	3325
Year n	Total Residential Wireless Grids	3901	0	244	358	4502
	Total Institutional Wireless Grids	731	0	122	49	902
	Total WG (Residential + SME)	4632	0	366	406	5404
Results						
Year 1	CAPEX costs	541.324 €	- €	32.937 €	35.905 €	610.166 €
	OPEX costs	31.577 €	- €	2.030 €	2.234 €	35.840 €
Year n	CAPEX costs	29.302 €	- €	1.783 €	1.942 €	33.028 €
	OPEX costs	1.707 €	- €	110 €	121 €	1.938 €
Total	CAPEX costs	874.994 €	- €	53.246 €	58.033 €	986.273 €
	OPEX costs	51.033 €	- €	3.281 €	3.611 €	57.924 €

With the definition of the previous parameters our model calculate the wireless grids CAPEX and OPEX costs for each access network (the scenario is divided into 4 access networks) and for the study period (in this scenario the period is 15 years).

6 Conclusions

The evolution of computing and communication networks toward decentralized and distributed systems implies that all the intelligence is on the edge nodes of the networks. Integrating wireless devices with the traditional wired grid infrastructure will allow the access (transfer, processing, etc) to the information that is now scattered across the different devices.

This paper proposes a new architecture to integrate the wireless grids networks with the broadband access networks. The produced results can analyze how the costs vary from region to region, calculating the cost per user, cost per homes passed, payback period, NPV, IRR, end cash balance, CAPEX, OPEX, and so on. The proposal tool performs a detailed comparison of the different broadband access technologies in several scenarios. For each access network, the model chooses the best solution, based in the output results.

References

[1] Yong-Hyuk, M., Tran, M.T., Chan-Hyun, Y., Heyon-Sun, S., Jung-Yeop, J.: Wireless Grid Middleware Architecture for Providing Reliable Services, pp. 1–6 (2005)
[2] McKnight, L.W., Lehr, W., Howison, J.: Coordinating User and Device Behavior in Wireless Grids. In: Fitzek, F., Katz, M. (eds.) Cognitive Wireless Networks, pp. 679–697. Springer, Netherlands (2007)

[3] Srinivasan, S.H.: Pervasive wireless grid architecture, pp. 83–88 (2005)

[4] Pereira, J.P., Ferreira, P.: Access networks for mobility: A techno-economic model for broadband access technologies. In: 5th International Conference on Testbeds and Research Infrastructures for the Development of Networks & Communities and Workshops, Tridentcom, pp. 1–7 (2009)

[5] Pereira, J.P.: Broadband Access Technologies Evaluation Tool (BATET). Technological and Economic Development of Economy XIII(4), 288–294 (2007)

[6] Sarrocco, C., Ypsilanti, D.: Convergence and Next Generation Networks. In: OECD, CISP (2007)/Final (June 2008)

[7] Vittore, V.: Broadband in High-Growth Economies. In: Lartigue, J.-P. (ed.) Breaking the Barriers - Transformation to the Digital Life, pp. 317–324. Alcatel- Lucent's (2008)

[8] Wellen, J.: High-Speed FTTH Technologies in an Open Access Platform - the European MUSE Project. In: Lin, C. (ed.) Broadband Optical Access Networks and Fiber-to-the-Home: Systems Technologies and Deployment Strategies, pp. 139–166. John Wiley & Sons, Chichester (2006)

[9] McKnight, L.W., Sharif, R.M., Wijngaert, L.: Wireless Grids: Assessing a New Technology from a User Perspective. In: Designing Ubiquitous Information Environments: Socio-Technical Issues and Challenges, pp. 169–181. Springer, Boston (2005)

[10] Benedict, S., Rejitha, R.S., Vasudevan, V.: Threshold Accepting Scheduling Algorithm for Scientific Workflows in Wireless Grids, 1st edn., pp. 686–691 (2008)

[11] McKnight, L.W., Howison, J., Bradner, S.: Guest Editors' Introduction: Wireless Grids–Distributed Resource Sharing by Mobile, Nomadic, and Fixed Devices. IEEE Internet Computing 8(4), 24–31 (2004)

Implementation of Random Linear Network Coding Using NVIDIA's CUDA Toolkit

Péter Vingelmann[1] and Frank H.P. Fitzek[2]

[1] Budapest University of Technology and Economics
[2] Aalborg University, Department of Electronic Systems

Abstract. In this paper we describe an efficient GPU-based implementation of random linear network coding using NVIDIA's CUDA toolkit. The implementation takes advantage of the highly parallel nature of modern GPUs. The paper reports speed ups of 500% for encoding and 90% for decoding in comparison with a standard CPU-based implementation.

Keywords: Random Linear Network Coding, GPGPU, CUDA, parallelization.

1 Introduction and Motivation

Network coding is a relatively new research area, as the concept was just introduced in 2000 by Ahlswede, Cai, Li, and Yeung [1]. A large number of research works have been carried out looking into the different aspects of network coding and its potential applications in practical networking systems [7], [9], [10]. The authors in [3] provide an excellent summary of network coding. A brief definition of linear network coding could be: intermediate nodes in a packet network may send out packets that are linear combinations of previously received information.

This approach may provide the following benefits: i.) improved throughput, ii.) high degree of robustness, iii.) lower complexity and iv.) improved security.

As any other coding scheme, network coding can be used to deal with losses. In addition to that, network coding offers the possibility to recode packets at any intermediate node in the network. Traditional coding schemes only work end-to-end, so this is a unique feature of network coding which can be of great help whenever packet flows are intersecting as in fixed or meshed wireless networks. The potential advantages of using network coding are discussed in detail in [4], [6].

As stated beforehand the basic concepts of network coding has been shown in many research works. But only a small number of them considered the actual implementation of network coding together with complexity and resource constraints. Linear network coding requires enhanced computational capabilities and additional memory at the network nodes. The idea would be to utilize cheap computational power to increase network efficiency, as Moore's law suggests that processing power is becoming less and less expensive. However, the computational overhead introduced by network coding operations is not negligible and has become an obstacle to the real deployment of network coding.

T. Doulamis et al.: (Eds.): GridNets 2009, LNICST 25, pp. 131–138, 2010.

In our previous paper [12] we suggested to use the Graphics Processing Unit (GPU) for network coding calculations. We introduced a shader-based solution which yielded reasonably high throughputs. However, other GPU-based alternatives are also worth investigating.

The ideal solution would be to use a standard language and framework for GPU computing which is supported on a wide range of platforms. There exists an open standard for parallel programming of heterogeneous systems, it is called OpenCL (Open Computing Language) [5]. It is a framework for writing programs that execute across heterogeneous platforms consisting of CPUs, GPUs, and other processors. But right now, OpenCL is nothing more than a specification, since the standard has not been implemented yet (although both major GPU manufacturers, AMD and NVIDIA, have decided to fully support OpenCL in the future).

There is another solution which is currently available: NVIDIA offers a general purpose parallel computing toolkit called Compute Unified Device Architecture (CUDA) [2]. Although this toolkit can provide a very good performance, it has a major disadvantage: it only supports the last few generations of NVIDIA GPUs. This paper will introduce a CUDA-based implementation of Random Linear Network Coding (RLNC).

This work is organized as follows. Section 2 briefly describes the process of network coding. Section 3 provides an overview of NVIDIA's CUDA toolkit. Section 4 presents our CUDA-based implementation. Section 5 contains some measurement results, and Section 6 concludes this paper.

2   Concept of Random Linear Network Coding

The process of Network Coding can be divided into two separate parts, the encoder is responsible for creating coded packets from the original ones and the decoder transforms these packets back to the original format. The data to be sent can be divided into packets and a certain amount of these packets forms a generation. The whole data could be divided into several generations. The generation is a series of packets that are encoded and decoded together.

During encoding, linear combinations of data packets are formed based on random coefficients. All operations are performed over a Galois Field, in our case this is $GF(2^8)$. Let N be the number of packets in a generation, and let L be the size (in bytes) of a single data packet. Each encoded packet contains a header (L bytes) and a payload (N bytes), the aggregate size is $N+L$ bytes. At least N linearly independent encoded packets are necessary to decode all the encoded data at the decoder side. There is a slight chance that the generated random coefficients are not linearly independent, thus the decoding needs additional encoded packets to be completed. The decoding itself can be done using a standard Gaussian elimination.

2.1   The Encoding Mechanism

After reading N number of L sized messages, the encoder is ready to produce encoded packets for this generation. The original data ($N{\times}L$ bytes) is stored in a matrix of corresponding dimension (matrix B on Figure 1).

Random coefficients are also necessary for the encoding process. Each encoded packet requires N coefficients, i.e. N random bytes. For an entire generation we need $N{\times}N$ bytes which are also stored in a matrix (matrix C on Figure 1).

The payload of each encoded packet is calculated by multiplying the header as a vector with the data matrix. This operation can be realized with simple array lookups and xor operations (as described later). Basically, encoding is a matrix multiplication performed in the GF domain, as it is depicted on Figure 1.

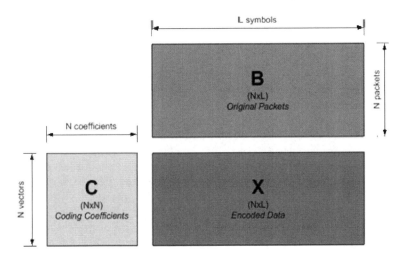

Fig.1. Encoding process in a matrix form

2.2 The Decoding Mechanism

The decoding algorithm used here is called Gauss-Jordan elimination which is basically an on-the-fly version of the standard Gaussian elimination. The encoded packets from the same generation are aggregated together, containing both the header and the payload part. Upon receiving a coded packet, the received data is being interpreted by using the previously received data. The elimination is based on the header part of the coded packet, but the corresponding operations are also performed on the payload part. The decoder stores the received, and partially decoded, data in an $N{\times}(N{+}L)$ sized decoding matrix. After the forward substitution part of the elimination each packet which carries new information will have a leading column in the header part with a non-zero pivot element, let's mark this column with K. This row is then normalized by dividing all of its elements by the leading value. After this step the new row can be inserted into the decoding matrix to the corresponding row (row K). The last step is to propagate this row back to the existing non-zero rows. The algorithm stops when the matrix does not have any empty rows, thence the header part forms an echelon form, and the payload part contains the decoded data in order.

3 NVIDIA's CUDA Toolkit

State-of-the-art 3D accelerator cards can be used to perform complex calculations, although they were originally designed to render 3D objects in real-time. A new concept is to use a modified form of a stream processor to allow a General Purpose Graphics Processing Unit (GPGPU) [8]. This concept turns the massive computational power of a modern graphics accelerator's shader pipeline into general-purpose computing power. On recent NVIDIA GPUs, it is possible to develop high-performance parallel computing applications in the C language, using the *Compute Unified Device Architecture* (CUDA) programming model and development tools [2]. GPUs have evolved into highly parallel, multi-threaded, multi-core processors. Unlike CPUs, which are originally designed for sequential computing, the design of GPUs is based on the *Single Instruction Multiple Data* (SIMD) architecture. It means that at any given clock cycle, multiple processor cores execute the same instruction, but they can operate on different data. The multiprocessor creates, manages, and executes concurrent threads in hardware with zero scheduling overhead. This allows a low granularity decomposition of problems by assigning one thread to each data element (such as a pixel in an image or a cell in a grid-based computation). The multiprocessor maps each thread to one scalar processor core, and each scalar thread executes independently with its own instruction address and register state.

In the CUDA model, the GPU is regarded as a data-parallel co-processor to the CPU. In CUDA terminology, the GPU is called *device*, whereas the CPU is called *host*. The device can only access the memory located on the device itself. A function executed on the device is called a *kernel*. A kernel is executed in the *Single Program Multiple Data* (SPMD) model, meaning that a user-specified number of threads execute the same program. Threads are organized into thread blocks which can have at most 512 threads. Threads belonging to the same thread block can share data through shared memory and can perform barrier synchronization. Furthermore, thread blocks can be organized into a grid. It is not possible to synchronize blocks within a grid. Thread blocks are required to execute independently: It must be possible to execute them in any order, in parallel or in series. This independence requirement allows thread blocks to be scheduled in any order across any number of cores, enabling programmers to write scalable code. The number of thread blocks in a grid is typically dictated by the size of the data being processed rather than by the number of processors in the system, which it can greatly exceed. The basic scheduling unit in CUDA is called *warp*, which is formed by 32 parallel threads. A multiprocessor unit is only fully utilized if all 32 threads in the warp have the same execution path. If the threads in a warp have different execution paths due to conditional branching, the instructions will be serialized, resulting in long processing time. Threads should be carefully organized to achieve maximum performance.

4 Implementation

The fundamental question is how to realize the Galois Field arithmetics in CUDA. If the field size is a power of 2, then addition and subtraction in the Galois Field are identical with the exclusive OR (XOR) operation, and this can be performed natively on the GPU. On the other hand, multiplication and division are more complicated over GF(2^8). These operations can be performed procedurally using a loop-based approach. However, it would not be efficient to compute the results every single time, a lot of clock cycles would be wasted this way. The other solution is to pre-calculate the results and store them in tables. The field size is 2^8=256, so the multiplication and division tables occupy *256x256 bytes* = *65 kB* each. These tables can be stored in graphics memory, and they can be bound to CUDA texture references to facilitate fast array look-ups. Two-dimensional texture coordinates are used to pinpoint a specific texture element which is the result of the multiplication or division.

4.1 Encoding

The encoding process can be considered as a highly parallel computation problem, because it essentially consists of a matrix multiplication in the GF domain. A parallel implementation is possible with little or no communication and synchronization among threads. Encoding of multiple coded packets - and even different sections of the same coded packet - can proceed in parallel by using a large number of threads. In CUDA, the GPU can only access the graphics memory, so all the coefficients and original packets have to be transferred from the host to the graphics memory first. Similarly, encoding results residing in graphics memory need to be transferred back to system memory. This imposes an additional overhead, but fortunately CUDA provides very efficient memory management functions.

The most essential design question here is how to partition the encoding task among the threads. We could launch one thread per coded packet (i.e. N threads for a generation), but this approach is simply not parallel enough. We can achieve higher performance with a much finer granularity, with each GPU thread encoding only a single byte of the coded packet, rather than working on an entire packet. This way $N \times L$ threads are necessary for encoding a whole generation. Performance improves significantly because GPUs are designed to create, manage, and execute concurrent threads with (almost) zero scheduling overhead.

The next measure towards further optimization is to process original packet data in 4-byte chunks, rather than byte–by–byte. Thereby we can reduce the number of memory accesses on the GPU. Each thread is responsible for computing a 4-byte chunk (i.e. a 32-bit integer) of the resulting encoded packets. Thus, we need $N \times L / 4$ threads for a whole generation. The CUDA-based encoding implementation uses random coefficients generated by the CPU, and transferred to the graphics memory before the start of the encoding process. Using this approach it is possible to compare the CUDA computation results with the reference results computed by an equivalent CPU-based implementation.

4.2 Decoding

The decoding process has a higher computational complexity than encoding. This leads to a reduced decoding performance in general. The efficient parallelization of the decoding process is a real challenge in CUDA. The fundamental problem with the Gauss-Jordan elimination is that the decoding of each coded packet can only start after the decoding of the previous coded packets has finished, i.e. it is essentially a sequential algorithm. Parallelization is only possible within the decoding of the current coded packet, and not across the whole generation as with the encoding process. The GPU needs to run thousands of threads to be able to achieve its peak performance, consequently the performance gain of GPU-based decoding is limited.

We receive each coded packet along with its associated coefficients (i.e. the encoding vector) and decode it partially. After receiving and decoding the N linearly independent coded packets, the decoding process completes and all the original packets are recovered.

For every new coded packet, we can partition the aggregate $N+L$ coefficients and data, such that each byte of the aggregate data is assigned to a thread, leading to a total of $N+L$ threads. Each thread reduces the leading coefficients of the new coded packet through a number of linear combinations. We multiply the previously decoded packets so that their leading coefficient matches the corresponding coefficient in the newly arrived coded packet. This way we can reduce a few of its coefficients to zeros. This multiplication-based approach can be parallelized, because we can reduce each coefficient using only the initial values of the other coefficients.

After completing this reduction step, a global search for the first non-zero coefficient becomes necessary. It is most likely that the position of this pivot element will match the current rank of the decoding matrix, but we cannot be sure about this. Running this global search is a major issue, since CUDA's synchronization construct only works for threads within a single thread block (max. 256 threads), and not among all GPU threads, therefore we are forced to perform this synchronization at the CPU side. This effectively breaks the decoding process into two separate CUDA kernels. Of course, if we want to develop a fully GPU-based solution for decoding, we could omit the CPU-side synchronization by introducing a new CUDA kernel for finding the pivot element. But it could run in only one thread, so there is no real benefit in doing this. Also note that launching another kernel means additional overhead, i.e. lower performance.

After finding the first non-zero coefficient at the CPU side, we launch another CUDA kernel to perform the remaining decoding operations, i.e. the backward substitution. But if we cannot find the pivot element (i.e. all coefficients were reduced to zeros), then the packet was linearly dependent, hence it is not necessary to launch this second kernel. The backward substitution part can be easily parallelized: we can assign a thread to each affected element of the decoding matrix (we should consider only the non-zero rows). This approach leads to a total of $N \times (N + L)$ threads when we process the very last packet of a generation, otherwise this number can be lower.

The first task of this second kernel is to normalize the reduced packet, and subsequently insert it into the decoding matrix. If the actual thread's index points to the correct row, the thread simply inserts the normalized data to that position. Otherwise, it has to perform a linear combination: we multiply the normalized packet with the coefficient at the pivot position in the current row, then this row is xored with this product. Note that each GPU thread affects only one byte of the decoding matrix. Extra care must be taken when we manipulate the coefficients at the pivot position in each row. Because the relative execution order of threads is not known, the initial values of these coefficients (i.e. one column of the decoding matrix) must be saved into a separate array. Thereby we can guarantee correct computation results.

5   Results

The following measurements are done on different GPUs with different generation sizes (N). The packet size is always equal to 1024 ($L=1024$). The following numbers indicate the measured throughput values in megabytes/seconds for encoding and decoding separately. Note that these are rounded averages of several measurements.

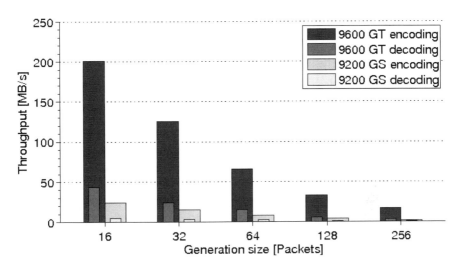

Fig. 2. Measurements performed on NVIDIA GeForce 9600GT and 9200M GS graphics cards

Note that the GeForce 9600GT can be considered a middle-class GPU, and the 9200M GS belongs to the low class. If we compare the results with the other implementations presented in our previous paper [12], then we may notice the significantly higher encoding throughputs. In some cases the CUDA implementation outperforms the CPU implementation by an order of magnitude, and it is twice as fast as the shader-based solution. The encoding algorithm is relatively simple, thereby its CUDA implementation can be considered straightforward, and we can obtain near-optimal encoding performance. On the other hand, the decoding throughput values are not significantly higher than those of the shader-based solution. This indicates that the current implementation is sub-optimal, so finding an optimal decoding solution for the GPU remains an open question for the future.

6   Conclusion

We introduced a CUDA-based implementation of Random Linear Network Coding which yields reasonably high throughput values. In fact, the numbers look promising compared to our previous implementations. We intend to port one of our GPU-based implementations onto mobile devices as soon as possible. At the moment, the GPUs on these devices lack certain capabilities required to run our application.

From a theoretical point of view, there is another interesting idea which might lead to simpler (and faster) implementations. The authors in [11] suggest that it might be beneficial to use a smaller Galois Field such as GF(2), despite the fact that the probability of generating linearly dependent packets increases significantly. On the other hand, the computational complexity decreases dramatically. Combining this idea with a GPU-based implementation can lead to very high throughput values in the future.

References

1. Ahlswede, R., Cai, N., Li, S.-Y.R., Yeung, R.W.: Network information flow. IEEE Transactions on Information Theory 46(4), 1204–1216 (2000)
2. NVIDIA Corporation. NVIDIA CUDA: Programming Guide, Version 2.0 (July 2008)
3. Fragouli, C., Le Boudec, J.-Y., Widmer, J.: Network coding: an instant primer. SIGCOMM Comput. Commun. Rev. 36(1), 63–68 (2006)
4. Fragouli, C., Soljanin, E.: Network Coding Applications. Now Publishers Inc. (January 2008)
5. Khronos Group. OpenCL - The open standard for parallel programming of heterogeneous systems (February 2009)
6. Ho, T., Lun, D.: Network Coding: An Introduction. Cambridge University Press, Cambridge (2008)
7. Katti, S., Rahul, H., Hu, W., Katabi, D., Médard, M., Crowcroft, J.: Xors in the air: practical wireless network coding. SIGCOMM Comput. Commun. Rev. 36(4), 243–254 (2006)
8. Luebke, D., Harris, M., Krüger, J., Purcell, T., Govindaraju, N., Buck, I., Woolley, C., Lefohn, A.: GPGPU: general purpose computation on graphics hardware. In: SIGGRAPH 2004: ACM SIGGRAPH 2004 Course Notes. ACM Press, New York (2004)
9. Matsumoto, R.: Construction algorithm for network error-correcting codes attaining the singleton bound E 90-A(9), 1729 (2007)
10. Park, J.-S., Gerla, M., Lun, D.S., Yi, Y., Medard, M.: Codecast: a network-coding-based ad hoc multicast protocol. IEEE Wireless Communications 13(5), 76–81 (2006)
11. Heide, J., Pedersen, M.V., Fitzek, F.H.P.: Torben Larsen: Network Coding for Mobile Devices – Systematic Binary Random Rateless Codes. In: The IEEE International Conference on Communications (ICC), Dresden, Germany, June 14-18 (2009)
12. Vingelmann, P., Zanaty, P., Fitzek, F.H.P., Charaf, H.: Implementation of Random Linear Network Coding on OpenGL-enabled Graphics Cards. In: European Wireless 2009, Aalborg, Denmark, May 17-20, pp. 118–123 (2009)

Collaboration in a Wireless Grid Innovation Testbed by Virtual Consortium

Joseph Treglia, Angela Ramnarine-Rieks, and Lee McKnight

School of Information Studies, Syracuse University, New York , USA
{jvtregli,auramnar,lmknigh}@syr.edu

Abstract. This paper describes the formation of the Wireless Grid Innovation Testbed (WGiT) coordinated by a virtual consortium involving academic and non-academic entities. Syracuse University and Virginia Tech are primary university partners with several other academic, government, and corporate partners. Objectives include: 1) coordinating knowledge sharing, 2) defining key parameters for wireless grids network applications, 3) dynamically connecting wired and wireless devices, content and users, 4) linking to VT-CORNET, Virginia Tech Cognitive Radio Network Testbed, 5) forming ad hoc networks or grids of mobile and fixed devices without a dedicated server, 6) deepening understanding of wireless grid application, device, network, user and market behavior through academic, trade and popular publications including online media, 7) identifying policy that may enable evaluated innovations to enter US and international markets and 8) implementation and evaluation of the international virtual collaborative process.

Keywords: Wireless and satellite networks, E-collaboration, Social and community networks, Infrastructures, Future ICT, Web based technologies, Security and safety.

1 Introduction

Syracuse University (SU) and Virginia Tech (VT) are creating the first Wireless Grid Innovation Testbed (WGiT) with the support of the National Science Foundation (NSF)[1]. It will help refine transformative technologies by bridging the gap between wireless network middleware and grid application layers, thus creating new markets and realigning existing ones. This will serve industry needs for intra-system, or cross-over work bridging grid or cloud computing on one platform and wireless Internet on another, contributing to open standards and application programming interfaces for wireless grids[2].

The uniqueness of this innovative testbed lies in its combination of new technologies for 'edgeware' for grid computing applications across edge devices, with wireless networking. The potential influence of this combination on current wireless

---

[1] This project is supported by the National Science Foundation (NSF) grants, NSF #0227879 and NSF # 0917973.

[2] Note that views expressed are those of the authors and not necessarily by the respective affiliated institutions.

T. Doulamis et al.: (Eds.): GridNets 2009, LNICST 25, pp. 139–146, 2010.

connectivity standards will be explored. The project will also investigate the wireless grids' utility to digital communities (including open source technical development communities) in being able to work and collaborate in a distributed, mobile fashion. Businesses, government agencies and private individuals will have new options for interacting and conducting business. The testbed provides students, faculty, firms and government representatives an opportunity to learn from and participate in the growth of this new market. This project will involve participants globally and permits easy access to its main findings and activities, thereby benefiting individuals, researchers as well as companies including media worldwide, in both developed and developing countries, spurring further innovation and economic growth on top of these NSF-derived technologies [1].

The primary goal of WGiT is to bring together unique technical assets from SU and VT, supported by National Science Foundation (NSF) grants, for further evaluation and to establish a baseline set of open or public interfaces, specifications, or standards, for wireless grids. Technical issues that are ripe for further research and analysis as part of this process will be supported by WGiT, including design and manufacturing, application performance and optimization, characterization of networks for wireless grid applications, and protocol development. Evaluation of service engineering simulations, user behavior trials, application tests, security models, and trust frameworks for wireless grids will be among the issues explored through the testbed, by faculty, students, and firms.

Innovaticus, a beta application undergoing testing through a SU campus trial, will be extended to VT and integrated with their own cognitive network testbed. Potentially there will be many more testbed partners within both universities and companies. This is but an early example of the type of products we expect to see more of over time.

A new virtual organization (VO), the Wireless Grid Testbed Consortium, is being created to manage the testbed and set the agenda and lead a globally distributed research effort on wireless grids - spanning the entire value chain from research, design, and manufacturing to consumer usage and policy. The establishment of WGiT promotes extended collaboration with other universities, industry members, and communities to share research and information, and spur innovation and economic growth. The outcome will be a better understanding of the key features of wireless grids (cognitive networks) enabling us to enhance the design, manufacturing and commercialization of the next generation of these information and resource (i.e., hardware, software, content) sharing innovations.

2 Background

The literature around the concept of national innovation systems incorporates a broad range of definitions, the starting point of which includes the "set of institutions whose interaction determine the innovative performance of national firms" [2], [3]. This reflected an important shift in academic understanding; away from linear models of innovation, to one more firmly grounded in policy frameworks. Freeman elaborated on the basic structure five years after Nelson's publication, including the network of institutions in the public/private sectors whose activities and interactions initiate, import, modify and diffuse new technologies [2], [4]. Others [5], [6], [7] expanded understanding of the 'triple helix' of industry-academe-government partnerships, with the latter explaining the interconnections between institutions as a driver of the store and transfer of knowledge, skills, and 'artifacts' that define new technologies. The need has been identified for access to knowledge as a key, critical catalyst for increasing innovative activities [8] [9]. This is placed squarely in the context of national economic development. Modeling tools shared and refined through WGiT may help researchers continuing to work on these challenges.

Wireless grids are defined as ad-hoc dynamic sharing of physical and virtual resources among heterogeneous devices. Recent relevant and related work regarding wireless grids include works on user and socio-technical perspectives and challenges [11], [12]; coordination of user and device behaviors [13]; future internet applications and bridging communicative channels [10], [14], [15]. There has been increasing acknowledgement of the nascent growth of wireless grids as a new engineering field of scientific inquiry and innovation [16]. The grid is an emerging infrastructure that will fundamentally change the way we think about and use computing [10]. A broader understanding of the nature of the opportunities offered by grid computing and the technologies needed to realize those opportunities is required [17]. The concept of a virtual workspace, as a configurable execution environment can be created and managed by reflecting client requirements [17], [18]. The development of WGiT will stimulate a variety of groups to use this technology in ways that are beyond their present understanding.

3 Project Description

WGiT seeks to evaluate specifications for possible standards in order to scale and integrate the 'transformative innovation' of wireless grids developed in a prior Partnerships for Innovation (PFI), together with specifications and protocols developed through the NSF I/UCRC Wireless Internet Center for Advanced Technology (WI-CAT), meshed with technologies and ideas from students, faculty, and companies worldwide. At SU, WGiT will test 'edgeware' or software that resides beyond the cloud, across edge network devices, both wired and wireless. At Virginia Tech, WGiT will also evaluate how such applications might perform on a recently established wireless cognitive radio network testbed (VT-CORNET). Technical standards and open application programming interfaces may be needed to enable this desired growth, and will be explored by the testbed, and discussed with project partners. Equally critical will be end-user feedback and systems and user evaluation.

3.1 Technical Development

This project continues efforts initiated by Tufts University, SU's Wireless Grids Lab, and spin-out firm Wireless Grids Corporation (WGC) under the prior PFI, to develop a technology that fills the need for better personal network usability, and standards for user-defined experience. The WGiT research agenda seeks to determine the extent to which wireless grid computing may successfully augment and enhance communication networks and standards such as the Internet, Bluetooth, WiFi, WiMAX and mobile WiMAX for data transmission, communication and collaboration. The wireless grid will enable shared resources among dynamic groups or social networks of computing and communication devices. Grids are comprised of objects and resources with individual profiles that are assigned a specific status relative to similar objects and resources. Services include multimedia recording; photo, printer, screen, connection and audio sharing; home monitoring, data storage and recovery, and integrated sensors and nanotechnology based devices.

3.2 Innovative Outcomes

There are many kinds of devices that can be shared, for example, mobile phones, mobile Internet devices, printers, displays, remote sensing devices, local weather sensors, wireless sensor networks, etc. Initially, investigation will focus on the software and hardware requirements for sharing wireless sensor networks for remote experiments under the wireless grid environment. Localization in a wireless ad hoc network is an important issue. There is no central control unit to identify the location of a node in a wireless ad hoc network. Location of a node can only be identified relatively to a node or nodes whose location is/are known. We have done localization research using signal strength to identify the node location. Power conservation is another important issue in mobile wireless network. A routing protocol for wireless network with power constraint has been developed. The signal strength of a transmission depends on the power of the transmitter. These two issues can be naturally considered and tied together in a wireless grid environment.

An interdisciplinary Electrical Engineering and Information Management senior capstone project will be developed using wireless grids for spring semester 2010 and will be taught jointly among SU, VT and Tufts University. We will teach a group of students how to use the wireless grid (at Syracuse) and a cognitive radio network testbed (at VT) to run a variety of applications for the wireless grid. Students from each of the campuses will be able to remotely deploy experiments on the network at the other campus. Each project group will consist of students from all of the three campuses. Participation from Portugal's Instituto Superior Tecnico, and a Portuguese next generation network testbed operated by UMIC may be integrated by the following year. They will implement a web based user interface capable of acquiring data from wireless sensor networks. Wireless sensor network data will be acquired through an Ethernet based base station and Java code will be used to parse collected information and display them. To do this project, students will learn TinyOS, Java, sensor network and wireless grid topology. Once familiar with the sensor network topology, they will design a program that will be capable of reconfiguring a wireless sensor network. This is done through writing new code instructions to the wireless sensors, i.e. reprogramming wireless sensors. Therefore they will write a program that can inject commands into a sensor network via the WGiT and we will run the localization application on the sensor network.

To allow students to share devices some preliminary solutions before the course will be explored and solutions will be articulated. At SU students in a variety of courses and through work at the associated labs will be provided with hands-on experience in the use of the wireless grid beta applications as they become available. The expectation is that in time, students will be able to easily develop their own wireless grid applications, building upon the platform provided. Through the testbed, students at participating institutions including high schools in participating communities will interact directly with each other and with engineers at the participating firms, as they design and use a variety of wireless grid applications as they are introduced, whether as proof of concept or prototype.

3.3 Entrepreneurship and Economic Impact by Design

The testbed itself is a new model for innovation and entrepreneurship to support economic growth. By fostering its "entrepreneurial ecosystem" around a VO supported by cyber infrastructure, we expect to refine technologies and standards to propagate wireless grid innovations across geographic locations, businesses and academic institutions. Interested government agencies and public-private partnerships at local, national, international and global scale, will contribute feedback.

Anticipated impacts to partnering firms include expansion and growth as markets emerge, first among partners and then more broadly across various vertical markets as students, faculty, firms – and governments – derive more strategic and precise applications of wireless grids that may fit their particular needs and interests. The testbed will support training and courses related to innovation, wireless grids technologies and business/social impacts opportunities, such as technology entrepreneurship offerings across campus.

From an enterprise perspective, our research and applications will potentially have the following impacts on businesses: 1) lowering transaction costs of internal knowledge and resource management, 2) lowering transaction costs of interaction with their customer base by enhancing and advancing how they communicate and offer their services, 3) increasing ROI by giving new capabilities to existing digital devices and networks, and 4) reducing total cost of ownership by enhancing remote service features.

3.4 Evaluation Methods and Outcomes

WGiT partners will integrate qualitative and quantitative feedback to monitor progress. For example we will achieve broader impact through information gathering around the core priority areas for the development community that we convene around the testbed as well as collect potential users' opinions regarding their needs.

Systematic evaluation and assessment as well as opportunities for unstructured feedback are essential for such projects to be useful and sustainable. Tufts and SU have been cooperating for several years in licensing the wireless grid innovations stemming from NSF PFI award 0227879. Pre-tests with SU's institutional review board (IRB) approval have been acquired, assessing data from an ongoing campus trial of wireless grid network, application, and user behavior. Pre-tests done in 2008 yielded valuable feedback from an initial user population on the SU campus. WGiT would expand this test across the Syracuse campus and into the community, and on to VT's campus.

VT's cognitive radio network testbed can be combined with the application and user layer data generated at Syracuse, yielding new insights into networks and applications from wireless grid specifications and future products. We propose using an epidemic model to evaluate the use and acceptance of Innovaticus and overcome barriers to acceptance that is limited by lack of information available about the new technology, how to use it, and what the technology does. Formalizing this diffusion process may enable firms to grow target markets within the wireless grid. Impacts of this work will be worldwide, as wireless grid products meeting specifications derived from the WGiT innovation testbed and integrating technologies from multiple partner organizations come to market. Immediate impacts will be observed in regional innovation networks and entrepreneurial ecosystems to both locally and internationally.

4   Collaborations and Partnerships

SU has joined forces with seven public and private universities in the New York State Grid project, a new venture to provide researchers access to high performance computing resources through the New York State Grid.

This PFI project involves an expansion of the wireless grid innovation testbed coordinated by SU and VT in partnership with several other academic, government and corporate partners. This will spur the growth of new companies and innovative services through the use of transformative developments in grid computing capabilities. The testbed will extend beyond small collaborations and individual departments in New York and Virginia to encompass wide-ranging and geographically dispersed activities and groups. The testbed aims at facilitating people-to-people, people-to-resources, and people-to-facilities interactions. This project will bring in Virginia Tech's College Engineering, and specifically the NSF IUCRC Wireless Internet Center for Advanced Technology (WICAT) to build upon the strong technical, industrial and institutional relationships built up over time, to manage the proposed WGiT. WICAT@VT is a subset of the world-renowned wireless center called Wireless@VT, which will bring in expertise in cognitive radios, wireless networking and other communications technologies.

A consortium will be created out of our partnerships and collaborations that will operate as an independent VO, with a paid membership of qualified universities and firms and led by both SU and VT Affiliated public agencies and community organizations and individuals will participate through local nodes of activity, namely the testbeds and beta trials in Virginia and New York, and the Instituto Superior Tecnico – Lisbon's research on the UMIC (Portuguese government) and EU-funded Next Generation Network community testbeds and modeling tools project.

The goal of promoting Wireless Grids is to see this functionality reach a much wider mass of people who do not have this level of technical knowledge. As technological innovation becomes centered on intuitive, easy access to the content, applications and devices [19], [20], [21], [22]; platform usage, user behaviors, user responses, and old/new applications will be monitored and analyzed by the Wireless Grids Research Lab and its WGiT partners.

5   Conclusion

Better assessment of wireless grids protocols and applications will inform design, manufacturing and commercialization of these next generation information and resource sharing innovations. The testbed will support training and courses related to innovation, wireless grids technologies and business/social impacts opportunities. The broader impact of the WGiT comes from the benefits foreseen from novel wireless connectivity standards and specifications; the wireless grids' utility to diverse digital communities (including the open source community) in being able to collaborate in a distributed fashion without network overload. Firms and government partners can help wireless grid innovations stemming from WGiT achieve national global impact. Ultimately, it will be up to its users and application developers, if WGiT is to achieve its intended broad impact on future education, technology, virtual collaboration and employment.

Acknowledgements

The development of the WGiT has been primarily funded by the National Science Foundation (NSF) under (NSF #0227879) 2002-2006 and will be continued under (NSF # 0917973) 2009. We are grateful for the continued support by our collaborators and partners at SU, VT, Tufts University, Norfolk State University Auburn University. Carnegie Mellon, MIT; Singapore National Technological University, Universidade Federal de Rio de Janeiro, Brazil, IST –Lisbon, University of Zurich and University of Aalborg. Also we note the cooperation of pioneering companies such as Qualcomm, Clear Channel Radio, and the non-profit defense and environmental systems contractor SRC (Syracuse Research Corporation) as well as small businesses SenSyr, MOD-E and WGC for considering adoption and/or production of these new applications.

References

1. McKnight, L.W.: Cognitive Wireless Grids: International Research and Education Testbed. NSF # 0917973 (2009)
2. McKnight, L., Vongpivat, P., Selian, A.: Mobile Regions: Entrepreneurship in Information and Communication Technologies in National Innovation System Models (2002)
3. Nelson, R., Rosenberg, N.: Technical Innovation and National Systems. In: Nelson, R. (ed.) National Innovation Systems: A Comparative Study. Oxford University Press, New York (1983)
4. Freeman, C.: Technological Infrastructure and International Competitiveness. Industrial and Corporate Change 13(3), 541–569 (1982)
5. Lundvall, B.-A.: National Systems of Innovation: Towards a Theory of Innovation and Interactive Learning. Pinter, London (1992)
6. Patel, P., Pavitt, K.: Large firms in the production of the world's technology: an important case of 'non-globalisation'. Journal of International Business Studies 22(1), 1–21 (1991)
7. Metcalfe, J.S., Hall, P.H.: The Verdoorn Law and the Salter Mechanism: A Note on Australian Manufacturing Industry. Australian Economic Papers 22(41), 364–373 (1983)
8. David, P., Foray, D.: Assessing and Expanding the Science and Technology Knowledge Base. STI Review 16, 13–68 (1995)
9. Bell, G., Callon, M.: Techno-Economic Networks and Science and Technology Policy. STI Review 14, 67–126 (1994)

10. McKnight, L.W.: The future of the internet is not the internet: open communications policy and the future wireless grid(s)" In. Washington, D.C.: NSF/OECD (2007),
    `http://www.oecd.org/dataoecd/18/42/38057172.pdf`
11. McKnight, L., Sharif, R., Wijngaert, V.D.: Wireless grids: assessing a new technology from a user perspective. Designing Ubiquitous Information Environments: Socio-Technical Issues and Challenges (2005),
    `http://dx.doi.org/10.1007/0-387-28918-6_14`
12. McKnight, L.W., Howison, J.: Toward a Sharing Protocol for Wireless Grids. In: International Conference on Computer, Communication and Control Technologies (CCCT 2003), Orlando, Florida, July 31-August 2 (2003)
13. McKnight, L., Lehr, W., Howison, J.: Coordinating user and device behaviour in wireless grids. In: Fitzek, F.H., Katz, M.D. (eds.) Cognitive Wireless Networks: Concepts, Methodologies and Visions Inspiring the Age of Enlightenment of Wireless Communications. Springer, Heidelberg (2007)
14. McKnight, L.W., Howison, J., Bradner, S.: Wireless grids–distributed resource sharing by mobile, nomadic, and fixed devices. IEEE Internet Computing 8(4), 24–31 (2004)
15. Dutton, W.H., Gillett, S.E., McKnight, L.W., Peltu, M.: Bridging broadband internet divides: reconfiguring access to enhance communicative power. Journal of Information Technology (2004)
16. Fitzek, F.H., Katz, M.D.: Cognitive Wireless Networks: Concepts, Methodologies and Visions Inspiring the Age of Enlightenment of Wireless Communications. Springer, Heidelberg (2007)
17. Foster, I., Kesselman, C.: The Grid 2: Blueprint for a New Computing Infrastructure. Morgan Kaufmann, San Francisco (2004)
18. Keahey, K., Foster, I., Freeman, T., Zhang, X., Galron, D.: Virtual Workspaces in the Grid. In: Cunha, J.C., Medeiros, P.D. (eds.) Euro-Par 2005. LNCS, vol. 3648, pp. 421–431. Springer, Heidelberg (2005)
19. Godin, B.: National Innovation System: The System Approach in Historical Perspective. Project on the History and Sociology of STI Statistics. Working Paper No.36 (2007)
20. Godin, B.: The Knowledge Based Economy: Conceptual Framework of Buzzword? Journal of Technology Transfer 31(1), 17–30 (2006)
21. Godin, B.: The Linear Model of Innovation: The Historical Construction of an Analytical Framework. Science, Technology, and Human Values 31(6), 639–667 (2006)
22. Lundvall, B.-A.: National Systems of Innovation: Towards a Theory of Innovation and Interactive Learning. Pinter, London (1992)

Challenges for Social Control in Wireless Mobile Grids

Tina Balke and Torsten Eymann

University of Bayreuth
Department of Information Systems Management (BWL VII)
Universitätsstr. 30, 95447 Bayreuth, Germany
{tina.balke,torsten.eymann}@uni-bayreuth.de

Abstract. The evolution of mobile phones has lead to new wireless mobile grids that lack a central controlling instance and require the cooperation of autonomous entities that can voluntarily commit resources, forming a common pool which can be used in order to achieve common and/or individual goals. The social dilemma in such systems is that it is advantageous for rational users to access the common pool resources without any own commitment, since every commitment has its price (see [9,13] for example). However, if a substantial number of users would follow this selfish strategy, the network itself would be at stake. Thus, the question arises on how cooperation can be fostered in wireless mobile grids. Whereas many papers have dealt with this question from a technical point of view, instead this paper will concentrate on a concept that has lately been discussed a lot with this regard: social control. Thereby social control concepts will be contrasted to technical approaches and resulting challenges (as well as possible solutions to these challenges) for social concepts will be discussed.

Keywords: Wireless Grids, Common Pool Dilemma, Social Control, Reputation.

1   The Common Pool Dilemma in Wireless Grids

Within the last years, the evolution of wireless and nano technology as well as computer networks have lead to a shift in ideas in the mobile phone world. Thus, not only are fourth generation mobile phones starting to place the user in the center of interest (user-centric view), but – associated with that – networks are evolving from centralized hierarchical systems with a centralized single management instance to decentralized distributed systems under the management of many [11].

Hence, Fitzek and Katz [8] for example, proposed to establish wireless mobile grids as shown in figure 1. In these wireless mobile networks, mobile devices with potentially different capabilities are envisioned to connect ad hoc and to cooperate and share their limited resources for the joint benefit. The cooperation between the mobile devices is enabled with the help of a short range

T. Doulamis et al.: (Eds.): GridNets 2009, LNICST 25, pp. 147–154, 2010.
© Institute for Computer Sciences, Social-Informatics and Telecommunications Engineering 2010

communication link, such as WLAN or Bluetooth. The advantage of this kind of communication architecture is firstly on the side of the resources. Thus, for example the battery power and CPU capacity needed on the short link is significantly lower than it would be needed on the cellular link making the concept advantageous from a resource point of view [7].

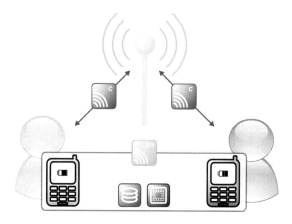

Fig. 1. Wireless Mobile Grid Communication Architecture [8]

However, despite the advantages, looking at the realization of the wireless mobile grid idea, from an economic point of view a problem appears that is very common to all open distributed systems in general: the network is depending on the cooperation of its users.

The cooperation idea in these networks is that, as shown in figure 2(a) the users voluntarily commit bandwidth, data storage, CPU cycles, battery power, etc., forming a common pool of resources which can be used either by all of them or in order to achieve a common goal [15]. The utility which users can obtain from the pooled resources is much higher than they can obtain on their own. For example, they can have access to a better variety of music, build a communication network, find solutions to complex computational problems in a shorter time, or achieve faster transfer of data to mobile terminals.

However, the problem in this constellation is that cooperation in these networks comes at a cost in the form of battery consumption, computation cycles, bandwidth or storage, etc. As a consequence, (bounded) rational users would prefer to access common pool resources without any own commitment, as shown in figure 2(b). Thus the yellow agent can enjoy the full benefits from the common pool without committing anything himself, i.e. by cheating on the three other agents. However, if a substantial number of users would follow this selfish strategy, the network itself would be at stake, depriving all users from the benefits [15].

The reason for this is straight forward: network users can have strategic behavior and are not necessarily obediently cooperating by making their resources

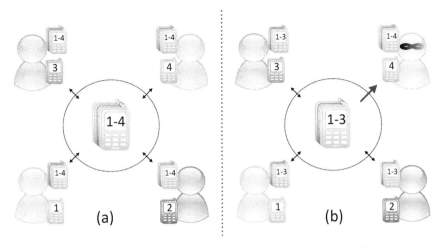

Fig. 2. The Common Pool Problem in Wireless Mobile Grids

available without the prospect of rewards for their good behavior. Unrecipro-cated, there is no inherent value of cooperation for a user. A lone cooperating user draws no benefit from its cooperation, even if the rest of the network does. Guaranteed cost paired with uncertainty or even lack of any resulting benefit does not induce cooperation in a (bounded) rational, utility-maximizing user. Rational users therefore would not cooperate in such an environment and all would be worse off than if they cooperated [1].

Consequently the question arises on how cooperation can emerge in such communication systems without any or with only rudimentary central author-ity where heterogeneous potentially selfish, bounded rational users with private utility functions act locally but their decision culminate in a global result?

2 Fostering the Compliance of Participants in Wireless Grids - Related Work

Scanning the scientific literature, there are four prototypical ways to foster coop-eration in distributed networks, namely technical, legal, economical and social ones [11]. Of these four, the two most prominent ones, namely technical and social concepts shall now be briefly explained and compared, as especially due to the very different basic concepts potentially promising implications for wire-less mobile grids may arise. Afterwards the paper will address social control mechanisms in more detail as these have recently been discussed at large as po-tential option to solve the cooperation challenge mentioned before. Thereby we will present a taxonomy of social control that is based on principal enforcement components and elaborate on challenges in each of the taxonomy elements.

2.1   Technical

Technical means are still the most widely researched approach to regulate behavior and foster cooperation. Thereby a methods is pursue which in social science is often referred to as regimentation: the appropriate behavior is "hard-wired" into either the network or if possible into the agents in the network through hard and software design. Typical examples of these technical means are communication protocols that are designed to limit the choice range of agents in order to cancel out non-system-conform behavior, or (especially in closed systems with non-human participants) the alteration of the mental state of the agents in the network to be in accordance with the normative system framework (this is done on the KAoS architecture [4] for example).

2.2   Social

The second common mean employed to foster cooperation in distributed and decentralized networks is based on social control mechanisms. As the name already implies, in these mechanisms the individuals of a society punish undesirable behavior and reward behavior that is in accordance with the goals of the system. Thereby two main approaches can be distinguished: the usage of cognitive components such as morality or conscience (i.e. the reflections of an agent about its own actions) or the use of social pressures (mostly in form of reputation) resulting from a group membership, in which others judge on the actions of an agent [11]. This group membership thereby can be as loosely as the common criteria of wireless mobile grid participation to a lot stronger ties like family membership. While both approaches help to increase cooperation, from a network designers point of view reputation seems more promising as the the cognitive impact on individuals can hardly be achieve. The basic idea behind reputation is that because people care about there reputation and because a higher reputation is supposed to yield higher long term income, they will not act in a way that may decrease their reputation and therefore they will cooperate in a system [14]. Contrasting reputation (and social mechanisms in general) to technical approaches, social mechanisms have the advantage to be independent of technological requirements. They do not need to be implemented beforehand, but can be applied and even changed and scaled at run-time making them more flexible and possibly less expensive from an implementation point of view. Furthermore social mechanisms are based on a number of information sources making attacks on the system less promising and the system itself more interesting for open distributed applications. However, as good as this may sound, there is a downside to social mechanisms as well. Thus, the distribution of information in the hands of many can lead to a distortion of information weakening the overall performance of social mechanisms if not implemented correctly.

Summing up, although social control mechanisms have some drawbacks that need to be discussed and solve in the future, they are one potential way (possibly together with technical mechanisms) to tackle the common good dilemma mentioned in the first chapter. That's why, in the further course of this paper, social mechanisms and especially the challenges connected with them will be placed in the main focus. Thereby, first of all the basic components of social control as seen by us will be presented to then go into detail about challenges for these mechanisms.

3   Challenges for Social Control

3.1   Social Control

Now that the two most common approaches for fostering compliance have been briefly presented, the paper will have a closer look at social mechanisms and their components with regard to cooperation. Thus, in our view, the social processes can be divided into 3 main parts that are relevant for enforcing cooperative behavior: (1) the definition of expected / allowed behavior, (2) the observation of the system in order to detect cheating (i.e. non-cooperative) behavior and (3) the application of sanctions in case a violation has occurred [6]. Whereas the definition of allowed behavior is normally externally given or evolves through time within the system, with regard to cooperation especially (2) and (3) are of interest. Thus, for social mechanisms there are 3 different kinds of observers that can be used in a system: first-party observers who control that their actions are in accordance with the rules in a system (whether self-imposed or imposed by other sources) themselves (these observers would correspond to the cognitive approach of social control), second-party observers who observe the behavior of their transaction partners and third-party observers that control the behavior of other agents the system. Looking at the side of the actual sanctioning, based on the observations, the same kind of enforcers are imaginable: social groups (up to the society as whole), second-party enforcers (i.e. the transaction partners) and first party-enforcers [2]. As a result of these considerations about (2) and (3), the taxonomy consisting of 4 main methods for social control that can be seen in the final column of figure 3 can be developed.

These four methods are:

- Social control with either second or third party observers in which – based on observation of parts of the society – the whole society (or groups of it) react to the violation. The best known example of this method are reputation mechanisms the are based on the information of single agents but due to the distribution of information result in social sanctioning by more agents than the one(s) not cooperated with.
- Promisee-enforced rules, i.e. mechanisms in which the agents not cooperated with punish the "cheater" themselves, e.g. in form of a "an-eye-for-an-eye" way or by not interacting with the same agent again.
- Self-control mechanisms that are especially interesting from a cognitive point of view. In contrast to all other mechanisms presented so far, it does not included any additional party, but only the agent performing an action itself. This agent is assumed to have an own normative value system and constantly checks whether his actions are in accordance with that own value system and

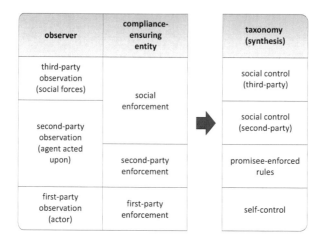

Fig. 3. Taxonomy for Social Control

the general normative wireless mobile grid framework (i.e. the agent is its own observer). Based on the normative value system the agent can then decide to sanction itself. An example of such a self-control scenario in wireless mobile grids could be that an agent that didn't contribute what he promised at a certain point of time is discontent with his performance (although the other agents might not have complained) and as a result offers the other agents something as compensation.

3.2   Challenges for Social Control Concepts

As the last step of this paper the specific challenges for social mechanisms will now be analyzed more closely. Thereby the four main methods derived at in the taxonomy will serve as a classification scene for the analysis. Hence, starting from the bottom of the taxonomy, challenges for each method as well as possible solutions will be presented.

Starting with the self-control method, the challenges this approach may have to face are very obvious. Thus, not only does this method leave the problem that it is dependent on the intrinsic motivation of the individual agents and thus it is not really to control from the outside, but furthermore it may pose an incentive problem. Assuming rational behavior, if no further changes are made to the system and the self-control method is the only way to foster cooperation, agents that act dishonestly will generate a higher profit than agents contributing to the system, crowding out cognitive cooperation effects. Some papers (see [3] for example) already address this problem by adding institutions that reverse the effect through adequate economic incentive mechanisms, however the model presented there only work for a limited parameter space and need to be further explored.

The second method, promisee-enforced rules, leaves the area of cognitive approaches and starts using weak social pressures instead. Thus, if being "cheated" second-party agents react themselves to the violation by storing their negative experience with the other agent (in social science this is often referred to as "image"-information [12]) and not interacting with the agent again. This reliance on own experiences has the advantage that information are always direct and correct, however due to the potential large number of other agents in a wireless mobile grid, the situation gets close to one-shot games in game theory, making the method very inefficient.

That is why in a last step, for the third and fourth method, the image information are circulated through the system either by the agent who was cheated or a third party who has witness the transaction. Although this might theoretical sound good, two major problems arise: the first one being the problem that false information might be generated by some agents and the second one being the problem that not enough information are contributed. This problem was dealt with by Conte and Paolucci [5] who distinguish 4 sets of agents (agents M transmitting an evaluation, evaluators E who evaluate the cooperation, targets T who are evaluated and the beneficiaries of the reputation information B, i.e. the agents who can use the information for their next cooperations. In their work Paolucci and Conte show that certain constellation of these sets of agents might either lead to wrong or to little evaluations. Looking at $E \approx T$ for example, i.e. a situation where the groups of evaluators and targets are highly overlapping (this is the case in the old eBay reputation mechanisms for example), "tit-for-tat" problems arise resulting in too good and too little reputation information. This idea was taken up by König et al [10] who could identified a certain constellation of the sets of agents for which enough correct reputation information is given and that consequently overcomes the problems just mentioned[1].

4 Conclusion

In this paper we looked at social control as one mean to overcome the common pool dilemma in wireless mobile grids. Thereby we first of all compared technical to social control mechanisms and pointed out the benefits of the latter. Afterwards, based on a taxonomy for social control, challenges were presented that need to be solved in order to establish social control in the long run. For these challenges, first approaches that try to address these challenges have furthermore been described. These approaches show that although still facing challenges, social control mechanisms are being worked on, nominating them as good complements for technical mechanisms in the future.

Acknowledgments. The work of Tina Balke was supported by the German Academic Exchange Service (DAAD).

---

[1] The constellation identified was $B \approx E, B \cap T = E \cap T = \emptyset$. For more information please refer to [10,5].

References

1. Axelrod, R.: The emergence of cooperation among egoists. The American Political Science Review 75(2), 306–318 (1981)
2. Balke, T.: A taxonomy for ensuring institutional compliance in utility computing. In: Boella, G., Noriega, P., Pigozzi, G., Verhagen, H. (eds.) Normative Multi-Agent Systems. Dagstuhl Seminar Proceedings, vol. 09121. Schloss Dagstuhl - Leibniz-Zentrum fuer Informatik, Germany (2009)
3. Balke, T., Eymann, T.: Using institutions to bridge the trust-gap in utility computing markets - an extended "trust game". In: Hansen, H.R., Karagiannis, D., Fill, H.-G. (eds.) Proceedings of the 9. Internationale Tagung Wirtschaftsinformatik, Vienna, February 2009, vol. 2, pp. 213–222. Österreichische Computer Gesellschaft (2009)
4. Bradshaw, J.M., Dutfield, S., Carpenter, B., Jeffers, R., Robinson, T.: Kaos: A generic agent architecture for aerospace applications. In: Proceedings of the CIKM 1995 Workshop on Intelligent Information Agents (1995)
5. Conte, R., Paolucci, M.: Reputation in Artificial Societies: Social Beliefs for Social Order. Springer, Heidelberg (2002)
6. Ellickson, R.C.: Order without Law: How Neighbors Settle Disputes. Harvard University Press (June 2005)
7. Fitzek, F.H.P., Katz, M., Zhang, Q.: Cellular controlled short-range communication for cooperative p2p networking. Wireless Personal Communications 48(1), 141–155 (2008)
8. Fitzek, F.H.P., Katz, M.D.: Cellular controlled peer to peer communications: Overview and potentials. In: Fitzek, F.H.P., Katz, M.D. (eds.) Cognitive Wireless Networks – Concepts, Methodologies and Visions Inspiring the Age of Enlightenment of Wireless Communication, pp. 31–59. Springer, Heidelberg (2007)
9. Kollock, P.: Social dilemmas: The anatomy of cooperation. Annual Review of Sociology 24, 183–214 (1998)
10. König, S., Hudert, S., Eymann, T.: Towards reputation enhanced electronic negotiations for service oriented computing. In: Proc. of the IEEE Joint Conference on E-Commerce Technology (CEC 2008) and Enterprise Computing, E-Commerce and E-Services, EEE 2008 (2008)
11. McKnight, L., Lehr, W., Howison, J.: Coordinating user and device behaviour in wireless grids. In: Fitzek, F.H., Katz, M.D. (eds.) Cognitive Wireless Networks – Concepts, Methodologies and Visions Inspiring the Age of Enlightenment of Wireless Communication, pp. 679–697. Springer, Netherlands (2007)
12. Miceli, M., Castelfranchi, C.: The role of evaluation in cognition and social interaction. In: Dautenhahn, K. (ed.) Human cognition and social agent technology. Benjamins, Amsterdam (2000)
13. Ostrom, E., Gardner, R., Walker, J.: Rules, Games, and Common-Pool Resources. University of Michigan Press (1994)
14. Sabater, J.: Trust and reputation for agent societies. PhD thesis, Institut d'Investigació en Intelligència Artificial, Universitat Autònoma de Barcelona (2003)
15. Wrona, K.: Cooperative Communication Systems. PhD thesis, RWTH Aachen (2005)

Author Index